My God!
He Is Magnificent!

And one of the elders saith unto me…behold, the Lion of the tribe of Judah, the Root of David, hath prevailed to open the book, and to loose the seven seals thereof. (Rev 5:5)

www.HeIsMagnificent.com

✳

Facebook.com/HeIsMagnificent

My God!
He Is Magnificent!

Devotional and Bible Study in Poetry and Prose

DEBBIE ADAMS

WESTBOW
PRESS®
A DIVISION OF THOMAS NELSON
& ZONDERVAN

Books of the Bible are referenced using the Three-Letter Abbreviation System. All abbreviations are three letters and in most cases the first three letters of the book name. Only five are abbreviated differently for clarification: Philemon (Phm); Philippians (Phl); Jude (Jde); Judges (Jdg); and Song of Solomon (Sos).

WestBow Press books may be ordered through booksellers or by contacting:

WestBow Press
A Division of Thomas Nelson & Zondervan
1663 Liberty Drive
Bloomington, IN 47403

www.westbowpress.com
(866) 928-1240

ISBN 9781512747133 (sc)
ISBN 9781512747126 (e)

Library of Congress Control Number: 2016910381

Print information available on the last page.

This is my gift to you, the Reader.
May this book bless you in a special way.

Oh some Scholar! Oh some Sailor!
Oh some Wise Man from the skies!
Please to tell a little Pilgrim
Where the place called "Morning" lies!

—Emily Dickinson
Excerpt from the poem:
Will There Really Be a Morning?

God's plan for enlarging His kingdom is so simple—one person telling another about the Savior. Yet we're busy and full of excuses. Just remember, someone's eternal destiny is at stake. The joy you'll have when you meet that person in heaven will far exceed any discomfort you felt in sharing the gospel.

—Charles Stanley

Watered down Christianity is nothing at all.
—C.S. Lewis

Table of Contents

Foreword

The Southeastern United States has been a garden of gifted writers, bringing literary nourishment to so many in so many ways. The gifted poets and writers who have come forth from this region are legion as well as legendary. Literature is a blessing and poetry a minister to the spirit of anyone persuaded to turn aside and find refuge.

A flower of that famous garden is someone I have had the privilege of knowing and sharing with. Debbie has given me a banquet of nutritious food for thought and provided ongoing encouragement as I move through life. She is someone who lives with enthusiasm the life God has provided and looks optimistically toward the day He has promised.

This collection of poems, essays and scriptural insights is from someone who loves and cares for her God-given audience. She makes no apology for being a follower of Jesus Christ in a time when people are acting as though they are ashamed to be so committed. This love is so powerful that it refuses to betray its origin. People like Debbie channel the Love of God naturally and share with patience and liberality.

Take your time with this collection and listen closely for the voice of God. There is a rich, nutritious harvest lovingly prepared for you. God bless you as you imbibe.

Steve McKee

Author, *Two Trees in the Garden*

Co-Author, *Poetic Synergy*

Acknowledgments

So we, being many, are one body in Christ, and every one members one of another. (Rom 12:5)

To Chris, my youngest son: Thank you for making it possible for me to publish my book and for your ongoing encouragement, insight, and support.

To Charles, my oldest son: Thank you for all your hard work on the design, layout, and editing of this book. Your input, patience, guidance, and many talents were invaluable.

And to Chuck Sr., my darling husband of more than 50 years: Thank you for being there and for your encouragement and helping hand in the whole process.

I could not have completed this book without you all. It was truly a family project. The Lord has blessed me mightily with such a loving, supportive, and caring family. I love you all without reservation.

About This Collection

I Jesus have sent mine angel to testify unto you these things in the churches. I am the root and the offspring of David, and the bright and morning star. (Rev 22:16)

My God! He Is Magnificent! is my first book of Christian poems and essays. It is a love story—pure and simple. Within these pages are pieces I have written over the years as I went about my daily living that express the passion and love I have for our Lord Jesus Christ. It is my way of honoring Him, as well as conveying my unfailing hope for His expected return.

Presented in a devotional and Bible study format, this collection depicts the Lord's multi-faceted presence throughout the Bible. Each poem and essay has Jesus at its center, reflecting His tender mercies and loving kindness, as well as His incredible power to shape every aspect of our lives.

As you journey through the pages of this book, my prayer is that it will help to enhance your awareness and understanding of our Lord, as well as direct you to the one true source of all such knowledge—the Holy Bible. If you are a believer and already know Him, I hope to share with you a special Christian camaraderie along the way. If you're still searching for answers, I would like to introduce you to our Lord so you can experience for yourself how magnificent He truly is.

There is no doubt: The Lord God of the Universe is very real and definitive! He is not a fictional, mythical, made-up being—nor is He some distant God Who remains aloof and uninvolved in our lives. Indeed not! Rather, He has chosen to have a personal relationship with each of us. Yes, our Maker and Creator knows our faults and foibles and yet He still loves and cares about us. No matter how insignificant you may feel, the Lord finds you precious and worthy in His sight!

For sure, you are never alone, for He is always there. If you let Him, the Lord will be with you throughout this life and beyond. He promised this to all who will believe in Him and sealed it with His sacrifice on the Cross.

Where God resides is not some far-away place. It is as close as your own heart. The Lord Jesus Christ has given you an open invitation. If you will only accept it, He will light up your life like the sun lights up the morning during a glorious, radiant sunrise!

My heart is inditing
a good matter:
I speak of the things
which I have made
touching the king:
my tongue is the pen
of a ready writer. (Psa 45:1)

The Writing Room

When I step into my Writing Room,
my pen draws words from ideas
as yet unformed.

In a fertile field of virgin thought,
the Word becomes the stem and leaf and blossom,
sown from the seed of proclamation,
to grow among the wild, untamed grasses
until it has reached a pre-determined height.

All sway in perfect rhythm with the Wind.
All remain in quiet unison
with the Spirit that dwells within.

In this place, not measured by
confines of time and space,
vivid ideas flow freely until,
in polished, printed form,
they are finished and complete.

From mundane thoughts,
fresh, full flowers of contemplation
burst forth upon the page in passionate expression,
opening freely to convey a caché of vibrant colors
that is the essence of my heart.

Briefly. Momentarily,
these abstract flowers bloom.
But, all too soon,
they wilt and fade.

Shortly, all will be gone,
but not all lost.
For, here in my Writing Room,
in my solitary space,
the evidence remains.

A lasting image
has emerged
on white sheet,
captured in
my words.

Foundation

In the Beginning, God...

In the beginning was the Word, and the Word was with God, and the Word was God...And the Word was made flesh, and dwelt among us, (and we beheld his glory, the glory as of the only begotten of the Father) full of grace and truth. (Joh 1:1, 14)

That Old, Old Story...

[Jesus said] I am the resurrection, and the life: he that believeth in me, though he were dead, yet shall he live... (Joh 11:25)

From Genesis to Revelation, we can find the glorious presence of our Lord in the pages of the ancient book we know as the Holy Bible. Indeed, the Scriptures in their entirety reveal the power, glory, and authenticity of our Lord as God and Savior. It's all part of "that old, old story" about the Son of God—Jesus Christ of Nazareth. This ageless story has been told and retold down through the centuries of recorded time to this modern day.

The Old Testament provides prophetic clues regarding "the Anointed One"—the "Messiah" Who would come at a future date. In contrast, the New Testament presents a factual, historical record of His life here on earth—where He was born, why He came, and Who He is, as well as the miracles and healings He performed. It also records His promise to "come again."

Without a doubt, when studying the Bible, the facts speak loud and clear. God directed the venerated writers of the Holy Scriptures to be purposeful and exact in their recording of these most sacred scrolls. The holy men who would later transcribe these Scriptures were just as careful and deliberate to record precisely the original Hebrew and Greek text. In much the same manner, those who translated these hallowed books into other languages—including Latin, German, and English—were also vigilant in preserving the original meaning.

When studying the Holy Scriptures, it is astounding to realize there are well over *three hundred* Old Testament prophetic passages that point to Jesus as the coming Messiah. Here are just a few examples:

1) His divinity in bodily form (Isa 9:6-7).
2) The exact location where He would be born (Mic 5:2-3).
3) The betrayal by a friend for precisely 30 pieces of silver (Zec 11:12-13, Psa 41:9).
4) A detailed description of how He would die (Psa 22).
5) The divine reason "why" He would die as He did (Isa 53).

When taken in total, the evidence is overwhelming. The Holy Bible clearly affirms the reality of Who Jesus Christ of Nazareth truly is. He is none other than the Lord God Jehovah, God the Son, the Second Person of the Holy Trinity, and Creator of the Universe. Yes, we can know with certainty that Jesus *was* God in the flesh and *is* Savior of the world! *God Himself* walked among the people, bringing healing, redemption, and eternal salvation to a lost and dying world. Most of all, He will return one day for those who believe in Him and take us to Heaven where we will live with Him forever.

Who hath measured the waters in the hollow of his hand, and meted out heaven with the span...Have ye not known? have ye not heard? hath it not been told you from the beginning? have ye not understood from the foundations of the earth? It is he that sitteth upon the circle of the earth...that stretcheth out the heavens as a curtain...Lift up your eyes on high, and behold who hath created these things, that bringeth out their host by number: he calleth them all by names... Hast thou not known? hast thou not heard, that the everlasting God, the LORD, the Creator of the ends of the earth fainteth not, neither is weary... (Isa 40: 12, 21-22, 26, 28)

For the invisible things of him from the creation of the world are clearly seen, being understood by the things that are made, even his eternal power and Godhead; so that they [who do not believe] are without excuse... (Rom 1:20)

Humanists would have us believe the Universe and the genesis of all life came about from one accidental, spontaneous, unintentional "explosion" somewhere "out there." They call it the "Big Bang Theory." And, that is exactly what it is—a theory, and one that is not based on sound logic or common sense reasoning. Yet, much like the theologians of centuries past who taught the earth was flat—even though the Bible speaks of "the circle of the earth" (Isa 40:22)—modern educators teach their "Big Bang Theory" as though it were proven scientific fact. In reality, it is not.

This theory is not even based on any type of reasonable mathematical odds. On a much smaller scale, it would be like believing a Boeing 747 could somehow appear fully formed and operational from the random rubble of a giant volcanic explosion. What are the odds of such a "Big Bang" bringing into being all the many various and sundry compounds and complex DNA structures needed for the billions of life forms here on Earth, much less those we don't yet know about out there in the Universe? Where did the atoms, particles, and raw components that supposedly exploded come from in the first place? Who created all that?

If we look around us at all the wonders of this world—the seas, the sky, the mountains, the grass, the forests, and all the creatures that live in each and every realm, not to mention how mankind was created with our ability to think, analyze, and reason —we can only come to one reasonable, logical, and rational conclusion. It is this: *There is a Creator.* He made the Universe in all its glory and placed us here on a planet in the "boondocks" of space and did so for His own purposes.

If that is the case, as far as the origins of the Universe and life are concerned, we must also conclude that science has it wrong. Therefore, where should we look for the truth regarding the origin of mankind and the Universe in which we reside? Ultimately, there is only one absolute, reliable source we can depend upon—not only regarding our origins, but also for *all* knowledge and wisdom. That source is the Holy Bible—God's Holy Word—passed down from the Creator Himself and presented to mankind as a *gift*—not only for knowledge, but also for "doctrine, reproof, and instruction in righteousness" (2Ti 3:14-17).

Bible Study: Gen 1:1, 17:1; Job 38:1-41, 40:1-24, 42:1-6; Ecc 12:1-2; Isa 40:2, 22-31, 43:14-17; Joh 1:1-5, 14; Rom 1:18-25; Rev 4:8, 11:17, 15:13, 16:7, 22:13.

To Doubters All

Logic and reason confirm absolutely
that only *nothing* comes from *nothing* and
will continue to be *nothing* into Infinity.

There can never *ever* be anything at all
unless *something* existed in the first place.

That *something* is the LORD God Almighty.
As it is written: "In the beginning, God..."[1]

1. Gen 1:1.

Hold fast the form of sound words, which thou hast heard of me, in faith and love which is in Christ Jesus. That good thing which was committed unto thee keep by the Holy Ghost which dwelleth in us. (2Ti 1:13-14)

...For we must all appear before the judgment seat of Christ; that every one may receive the things done in his body, according to that he hath done, whether it be good or bad. (2Co 5:10)

To understand the Word is to know Christ. Down through the ages, the Lord went to a lot of trouble to put the Holy Bible into the hands of individual Christians so we could read it for ourselves. Many believers died so we could have God's Word in our possession. Though the Holy Bible has gone through many generations and various and sundry translations, it has remained consistent and true. We should cherish the privilege of holding the Word of God in our hands.

There are several good, modern translations of the Bible in use today. For me, however, the most authentic is the King James Version. I consider it to be the "Rolls Royce Edition." Some think it is difficult to read and cumbersome to understand, comparing it to Shakespeare. The fact remains, however, it is still one of the most accurate versions in the world today. It is also the most widely read and memorized version of the Bible. For sure, none would argue the King James Version is the most beautifully written of all the translations. It is renowned the world over as a timeless work of art and remains one of the greatest literary classics of all time.

Yes, there will always be those who want to parse the words of the Holy Bible. They will accept what they want to believe and reject the rest. But, know this: The Bible is the *whole* truth. You can depend on it. When you read it and believe it, you will find God, and you will recognize Him for Who He is—the One Who Saves—Jesus Christ of Nazareth.

Whatever "authorized" Christian version you prefer, pick up your Bible today and make studying it a regular part of your daily routine. You will be blessed as you grow in the knowledge and wisdom of God's Word. It is a gift that keeps on giving—all the way into eternity.

Bible Study: Psa 18:3, 24:6, 80:3, 106:8, 107:13-15; Isa 43:12, 45:18-25, 63:7-16, 64:4-12; Jer 17:14; Mat 10:22, 19:25-26, 24:14; Mar 16:16; Luk 1:68-80, 7:44-50; Joh 3:16-21, 5:32-47, 10:7-18; Act 2:21, 4:1-12; Rom 5:1-21, 10:8-15; 1Co 1:18, 15:1-11; 2Co 2:14-16; Eph 2:4-10; 1Ti 2:3-6; 2Ti 1:9-10; Tit 3:3-7; 1Pe 4:18; Jde 1:24-25; Rev 22:11-21.

Saved or Lost?
It's Up to You

Our minds inject us
with ideas and thoughts.
Our words and actions
reflect what our minds have wrought.
But, it is our hearts alone that convict us
by simple faith,
and determine once and for all
our eternal state.
When you look upon that Cross,
will you be saved—
or forever lost?

How shall we escape, if we neglect so great salvation; which at the first began to be spoken by the Lord, and was confirmed unto us by them that heard him; God also bearing them witness, both with signs and wonders, and with divers miracles, and gifts of the Holy Ghost, according to his own will? (Heb 2:3-4)

Christianity is unlike any other religion in the world. It is the One True Faith. Other religions are sometimes called "faiths." In reality, however, they are not. Instead of believing "on faith," these other religions require all kinds of so-called "good works," as well as penances and pilgrimages, and sometimes even a particular birthright, social status, or ethnicity. Sadly, in all the other religions in this world, people readily accept the false notion that one needs to *earn* his or her way into Heaven.

In Christianity, however, we understand there is only *one* door into Heaven, and that door is Jesus Christ. There is only one way and one faith that will get you there. Jesus alone provides unfailing grace, mercy, and forgiveness (Joh 10:9). He tells us in John: "... I am the way, the truth, and the life: no man cometh unto the Father, but by me" (Joh 14:6). All the rest of the religions, ideologies, and belief systems in this world will guide you down paths that lead only to jagged cliffs of doom, despair, and eternal destruction.

The Lord God is the "real thing!" He is neither a myth nor a legend. He is not a "figment of our imagination." He is not whatever we imagine Him to be. We did not create Him. *He created us.* God is real, and He is *alive*—and has been from time immemorial. He is the same yesterday, today and forever (Heb 13:8).

The Lord God Jehovah came to us in the Personage of Jesus Christ of Nazareth. He walked the earth as a humble carpenter turned Rabbi. Jesus lived here as a mortal man for just thirty-three years, and yet He has been around for eternity, for He is the "Eternal Son." His presence on earth changed the world forever. History is recorded according to "before Christ" and "after Christ," i.e. B.C. and A.D. Recently, the secular world has changed this designation to B.C.E. and C.E., i.e. "Before the Common Era" and the "Common Era." And yet, they still can't change the important fact that our western culture and the entire world's historical timeline are directly based on Christ's life and His sojourn on this earth.

The only requirement to follow Christ is to believe Who He is and accept on faith the redeeming grace that He alone offers. Then, we ask Him to forgive our sins and humbly accept His grace. He will do the rest. Jesus saves us, changes us, and eventually takes us to Heaven to live with Him forever.

As Isaiah said, it's important to "seek the Lord while you can" and call on Him "while He is near" (Isa 55:6). Jesus has given you a choice: You must either accept Him or reject Him. The decision is yours. But, remember, your choice will have eternal consequences.

Bible Study: Psa 22, 23, 24; Isa 49:8; Mic 5:23; Mat 1:1-25, 4:4; Mar 1:15, 10:30; Luk 3:23-38, 4:4, 11:30, 12:2, 18:31, 20:18; Joh 1:1-3, 10, 14, 6:26-29; Act 2:22; Heb 2:3-4, 4:15; Rev 22:16-17.

The Day of Your Salvation

Hear the Word.
Matthew, Mark, Luke and John.
They are "God spell"— every one.
Listen to the Good News.

From these Gospels,
the real Word was heard,
and one true voice emerged—
the Voice of the living God.

Jesus said: ...*Man shall not live by bread alone,
but by every word that proceeds out of the mouth of God.*[1]

It was over 2000 years ago.
Jesus of Nazareth walked throughout Palestine—
as the one and only living Sign.

Jesus said: *For as Jonas was a sign unto the Ninevites,
so shall also the Son of man be to this generation.*[2]

These were the days of miracles galore,
in the desert and by the shore.
Those who saw Him—everyone—
wondered at all the great things He had done—
this man—the living Son of God.

Jesus said: ...*The time is fulfilled, and the kingdom of God
is at hand: repent ye, and believe the gospel.*[3]

How can anyone *not* believe that which is depicted
in the pages of Old and New Testament text?
It is not complex.
There is no convolution here. No trickery.
It is the simple Truth.

(Continued)

Jesus said: ...*This is the work of God, that ye believe on him whom he hath sent.* [4]

Jesus Christ, the Man from Heaven—
the One that *was* and *is* and *is to come*—
The One Who promised He will return.
As Man, He was conceived in the spiritual.
As God, He was incarnated in the physical.
Destined as the sacrificial Lamb,
He is the *Great I Am*.

Jesus said: ...*Behold, we go up to Jerusalem, and all things that are written by the prophets concerning the Son of man shall be accomplished.* [5]

Now, believe or not, it's up to you.
If you do, be still and take to heart the Word of God.
If not, depart, and be on your way,
remembering always that this day
could have been—*would* have been—*should* have been—
the day of your salvation.

1. Mat 4:4; 2. Luk 11:30; 3. Mar 1:15; 4. Joh 6:29; 5. Luk 18:31.

Fulfillment
Good Tidings of Great Joy

How beautiful upon the mountains are the feet of him that bringeth good tidings, that publisheth peace; that bringeth good tidings of good, that publisheth salvation; that saith unto Zion, Thy God reigneth! (Isa 52:7)

* * *

As for God, his way is perfect: the word of the Lord is tried: he is a buckler to all those that trust in him. For who is God save the Lord? or who is a rock save our God?...The Lord liveth; and blessed be my rock; and let the God of my salvation be exalted. (Psa 18:30-31, 46)

The Divinity of Christ

In the beginning was the Word, and the Word was with God, and the Word was God...And the Word was made flesh, and dwelt among us... (Joh 1:1,14)

In Old Testament times, the Lord God Jehovah spoke directly to His prophets. These words were carefully written down in the pages of ancient Scripture that make up the thirty-nine books of the Old Testament—from Genesis to Malachi. Then, God was silent for over four hundred years. As prophesied, however, the Lord did eventually speak once again to His people. This time it was in person, and His message was recorded in the twenty-seven books of the New Testament—from Matthew to Revelation. Eventually, this message would be sent to the far-reaching continents of the earth, starting in Jerusalem and spreading westward. Now, a little over 2000 years later, the Gospel of Christ has reached around the globe.

When the Lord God came to earth in the flesh, He walked the paths of Palestine as a humble carpenter turned rabbi. Jesus Christ of Nazareth spoke directly to the people and performed many extraordinary signs and wonders just as prophesied in the Scriptures. After His crucifixion and ultimate resurrection, Jesus' unparalleled message of mercy, forgiveness, grace, hope, and eternal salvation for a lost and dying world continued to flow from His disciples. This message, along with the record of His Virgin birth, extraordinary life, tortuous death, and miraculous resurrection, would eventually be documented in select books of what we now know as the New Testament.

Included in these holy pages are eyewitness accounts of the Lord's astonishing works written by those who had personally known Him. Through Christ's healing powers, the dead were raised, lepers were cleansed, cripples walked, the blind could see, and the deaf could hear. He also turned water into wine, walked on the sea, calmed a storm, and fed thousands from one small basket of loaves and fishes—not once, but twice. The miracles were so prolific, the Apostle John stated "if they should be written every one, I suppose that even the world itself could not contain the books that should be written" (Joh 21:25).

Since Jesus walked the earth those centuries ago, He has continued speaking to His followers—Christians—through the pages of the Holy Scriptures. For this very reason, God's written Word—the Holy Bible—is our core source of knowledge and standard of *truth*.

From the porticos, galleries, colonnades, and corridors of centuries past, the Almighty has proclaimed His identity for all to see. Indeed, the Lord Jesus Christ has made known the reality of His divinity as He calls us to come and follow Him. His Holy Word provides an oasis of clarity, consistency, and truth in a relativistic, ever-changing, confusing, and chaotic world.

In this one supernatural book that you can hold today in the palm of your hand, the Lord Jesus reaches out to all mankind, calling us to repent, come unto Him, and accept His amazing grace. He offers love, hope, solace, mercy, and redemption, bringing eternal salvation to a people lost in their own self-absorbed delusions and mortal sins.

Breaking the barriers of time, the Lord God speaks to generation after generation through the pages of the Holy Bible, revealing His awesome nature to those who will listen and understand. Most importantly, He offers each of us a *choice*—either to accept Him or to reject Him. In this way, our Lord gathers believers from all corners of the earth and will continue to do so until He returns.

Because I will publish the name of the Lord: ascribe ye greatness unto our God. He is the Rock, his work is perfect: for all his ways are judgment: a God of truth and without iniquity, just and right is he. (Deu 32:3-4)

Of all my poems, this has been one of the most popular among my family and friends. So many have told me it gave them great comfort in time of their own personal crises. I think the reason may be because it is a compilation of scriptural verses. We can receive no greater consolation and comfort in our time of need than from the Word of God. As we know from Scripture, it is "not by might, nor by power, but by my spirit, says the Lord..." (Zec 4:6).

This poem came about one morning as I was reading the Psalms in my daily Bible study. Suddenly, snippets of different passages from various parts of the Bible came flooding through my mind, and I wrote them down as fast as I could. As I was writing, I was overwhelmed at the awesomeness and magnificence of the Lord our God—all He is and all He has done. Even more, I was astounded by the significance of these Old Testament passages, for each applied to the many facets of Christ.

In both the Old and the New Testaments, passage after passage confirms that Jesus Christ of Nazareth, the Second Personage of the Trinity, is the fulfillment of Bible prophecy regarding the Messiah. He is God come to earth in the flesh to provide salvation to those who will accept Who He is and believe on Him. With God the Father as Abba ("Daddy"), with God the Son as our Savior, Advocate and Friend, and with God the Holy Spirit as our Comforter and Counselor, there is no greater consolation. We are in good hands: God in Three Persons—Blessed Trinity.

In Loving Memory:

My cousin, Carolyn Loretta Hinson ("Loby")

July 13, 1941 ✝ July 06, 2017

My friend, Wendy Joy Leathers

October 27, 1972 ✝ July 18, 2017

My niece, Brenda Joyce Flowers Keel

August 24, 1954 ✝ January 27, 2018

Bible Study: 2Sa 22:3, 31; Psa 18:30, 89:7, 91:4; Pro 2:7; Sos 8:5; Isa 19:20, 45:15, 49:26, 60:16, 63:16; Hos 3:14; Mat 1:22, 2:15, 17-18, 23, 4:12-17, 8:16-17, 12:14-21, 13:14-15, 34-35; Mar 15:28-29; Luk 1:46-47, 2:11, 4:21, 24:44; Joh 3:29, 4:42, 24-26, 17:12, 18:8-9, 31-32, 19:24-28, 36; Act 1:16, 3:6, 18, 4:10, 5:31, 12:37-41, 13:18-33; Rom 8:4-6; Jam 2:23; Php 3:20; 1Ti 1:1, 2:3, 4:10; 2Ti 1:10; Tit 1:1-4, 2:10-13, 3:4-7; 2Pe 3:18; Heb 3:14; Rev 1:8-11, 17:17, 21:6, 22:13.

The Lord God

The Lord is always before me.
In Him, my flesh rests in hope.
My trust remains steadfast. My faith unshakeable.
My heart glad. My spirit rejoicing.
I shall not be moved.

Only in the presence of the Lord
is there fullness of joy.
I will delight in His right hand forever more.
He will not leave my soul in Hell.
He will direct me on the path
to life everlasting,

He is the incorruptible, indestructible,
Perfect One that saves.
I call and He hears. I cry and He listens.
He liberally bestows upon me
His tender mercies and loving kindness.

He protects me from my enemies.
In whom shall I fear?
I am the apple of His eye.
His love for me has no bounds.
He hides me under the shadow of His wings.
He leads me in the paths of righteousness
for His name's sake.

I fall on my knees and pray.
Great is the Lord and greatly to be praised.
He is my Rock, my Fortress, my Deliverer.
He is my Buckler, my Strength, my Shield.
He is my Savior, my Counselor, my Friend.
In Him I can do all things. Without Him I am nothing.

Who is this mighty, glorious, Omnipotent One?
Jesus is His name.
He is Jesus Christ of Nazareth, Lord God of the Universe.
Did you not know? He is One and the Same.

References: 1Ch 16:25; Psa 4:3, 16:8-11, 17:6-11, 18:2-6, 23:3, 25:6, 40:11, 48:1, 55:16, 96:4, 103:4, 145:3; Isa 9:6, 43:3; Zec 2:8; Joh 15:13; Php 4:13; Jde 1:24-25; Rev 19:16.

Therefore the Lord himself shall give you a sign; Behold, a virgin shall conceive, and bear a son, and shall call his name Immanuel. (Isa 7:14)

When Christ first came to earth, He did not fit the false notions of what the Jewish priests and scribes thought the Messiah would be. Instead of a royal setting, Jesus was born in a manger. Rather than being the son of an earthly king, He was the son of a carpenter, growing up in the cultural equivalent of today's middle class. Until He began His ministry, Jesus led an ordinary, nondescript life. He was neither a warrior nor a triumphant king. Instead, He became a gentle rabbi, going about the countryside on foot preaching a new Gospel. Even after the Jewish elite saw how many Old Testament prophecies Jesus fulfilled, they still refused to believe.

It would seem an impossible task for any one man to fulfill the hundreds of requirements predicted in the Old Testament regarding the Messiah. The probability of *ever* satisfying all the scriptural prophecies is astronomical. In fact, the mathematical odds are way beyond the ability for most of us to calculate. Given Jesus' simple lifestyle, it would seem highly improbable for this particular young man to satisfy even one. And yet, He fulfilled *all* the biblical requirements related to His first coming and will complete the rest when He returns.

As the Son of God, this unassuming carpenter turned rabbi could have sat on the highest throne of the day and lived a life of luxury and comfort. Instead, He chose a humble existence, walking among His people and preaching the Gospel of faith, hope and love, salvation through grace, and eternal redemption to a lost and dying world.

All the while, Jesus knew how His time here on earth would end. As predicted, He would be betrayed by a kinsman. As predicted, He was whipped and scourged, and a crown of thorns was jammed onto His head. As predicted, He was nailed to a cross where those watching could see His nakedness and soldiers cast lots for His garments.

Why would God send His only Son to willingly die a horrible death for the salvation of sin-ridden mankind? He did it for you and for me and for all of us willing to accept His redeeming grace. As predicted, this was *not* the end of His story. It was only the beginning, for Jesus was resurrected from the grave. He now sits on the right hand of the Father in Heaven and will one day come again for His faithful followers—as predicted.

To all our dear friends in the *Grand Floridian Society Orchestra* at Walt Disney World and their families with love including: Bobby Pickwood and his wife, Pam, Dick Fote and his wife, Gail, and their families; To the "Cake Lady," Pat Anderson and Richard, the "Greeter"; To the *Pearly Kings and Queens* at EPCOT Center, Pat Terry and his wife, Judy, Charlie Borneman and his wife, Marsha, Connie Colgan, and Michelle Girard. Also, a special remembrance to our Disney friends who have gone on to be with the Lord and to their families: Lloyd Wooley, Lou Mauro, Lee Richardson, Skip Harding, Rick Fay, Billy Barnes, and Fred Edlund.

Bible Study: Gen 3:8-17, 4:16, 49:11; Num 24:17; Deu 10:17; 2Sa 7:12-16; Psa 2:7-12, 9:3, 22:1-31, 23:1-6, 24:1-10; Isa 7:14, 9:6, 49:8, 52:14, 53:1-12, 59:15-20, 61:1-2; Dan 9:24-27; Zec 9:9, 11:12-13; Mic 5:2-3; Mal 3:1; Mat 1:1-25, 4:4, 21:5-7, 24:31, 26:67-68, 27:3-4, 26-30, 57-61; Mar 1:15, 10:30, 15:42-47; Luk 3:23-38, 4:4, 11:30, 12:2, 18:31, 20:18, 23:32-46, 50-56; Joh 1:1-14, 6:26-29, 19:1-3, 38-42; Act 2:22-33, 13:33; Eph 2:12; Heb 2:3-4, 4:15, 10:12, 13:15-16; 1Pe 2:24; Rev 1:5, 11:15, 17:14, 19:16, 22:3-17.

Behold Your God!

We were not given life just to hold.
We were given life to *behold*
and to testify to the mighty, awesome presence
of God come in the flesh.

Behold! Our Savior, Jesus Christ,
the unblemished Lamb of Sacrifice.
He has paid the price to offer us eternal life.

Behold! God the Son,
the true and holy Righteous One.
On Calvary's Cross, He gave His life for a lost and dying world.

Behold Immanuel! Seek Him diligently while He can still be found.
He has the power to forgive. He has the power to save,
and He has the power to raise us up into Heaven.

Behold! The Lord of Lords and King of Kings.
Hallelujah and praise! He has risen from the grave!
Forever and ever Christ will reign. Glory to His name!

Behold your God! By His stripes, we are healed.
By His Spirit we are sealed.
He is Alpha and Omega, the Beginning and the End.
If you haven't already, won't you come unto Him?

And Jesus said unto them...If ye have faith as a grain of mustard seed, ye shall say unto this mountain, Remove hence to yonder place; and it shall remove; and nothing shall be impossible unto you. (Mat 17:20)

No matter what our needs, we should learn to have faith like Peter had during those few moments out on the stormy sea. If our faith is just the size of a tiny mustard seed, the Lord says we can move mountains. Think about it. A mustard seed is 1-2 millimeters in size and there are 25 millimeters in an inch. That's how small it is. That's all the faith we need to move a mountain—just a "tiny smidgen."

Just the other day, my oldest son, Charles, and I were in an outlet mall. He was complaining how crowded it was, saying we probably wouldn't be able to find a parking space near the store where I needed to go. I have difficulty walking so when I'm with either of my two sons, they always park as close as possible to the store. They are both considerate that way.

Unfortunately, all the handicapped spaces were taken so we were left to find a spot in the great, big wide parking lot full of automobiles. I reminded Charles that all he had to do was "pray," and we would find just the right one. "You need faith like Peter had when he walked on water." He looked at me sideways and said, "You pray. I'm driving." So, I bowed my head and said a quick prayer. Sure enough, right in front of the store, a car started backing out. I smiled at him. Actually, I beamed. He shook his head and smiled back at me while he waited to pull into our newly found parking space.

This has been a game with my two sons and me since they were little. In one respect, it was a way of teaching them to depend on the Lord for everything. My youngest son, Chris, took it to heart. Now, as an adult, he's like me in that he almost always finds a parking space when he needs it. Charles, however, still has a tendency to focus too much on the circumstances—how crowded it is, the time of day, etc. Add to that, he doesn't think we should really "bother the Lord" about such small things.

Interestingly, time and again, he'll have trouble finding a parking space. So, I still have to remind him on occasion that, even in the smallest things, we should focus on the Lord and not on our circumstances. Peter walking on water was a good example of this. Once he took his eyes off Jesus, he began to sink!

Of course, finding a parking space is quite insignificant in the scheme of things, but the principle is still the same. Even in our mundane daily lives, we should learn to focus on Jesus for *all* our needs—no matter how insignificant. It's good training for those "storm-tossed times" when we really need that little seed of faith in our lives to "move mountains" or "walk on water"—spiritually speaking that is.

To our dear friends, Patricia and Doug and their family with love.
Trish, you are my dearest friend from youth.
Whether it's a parking space or getting stuck in the sand on the beach,
praying out loud works every time.

A lifetime's not too long to live as friends...
—*Friends Are Friends Forever*, Song by Michael W. Smith

Bible Study: Mat 14:24-33, 17:20; Mar 4:31, 6:45-52, 11:21-26; Luk 17:6; Joh 6:16-21.

Faith the Size of a Mustard Seed

Faith, the size of a mustard seed.
Tiny. Infinitesimal. Miniscule. Small.
With it grasped tightly in the ball of his fist,
Peter the Fisherman walked on water.

Burly. Boisterous. Warrior. Leader.
That was Peter, the disciple who would later
cut off the Temple guard's ear to save his Master.
He remained near his Lord *until*—
but then later *still*—well, you *remember*.

How bold! How gallant! How valiant!
If Jesus could walk on water,
so could he! And, he did!
But, only for a moment.

Then, Peter took his eyes off Jesus,
eyeing the storm instead.
Oh God! What a sight!
The endless churning Sea of Galilee.
Thunderous lightning bolts flashing.
Furious waves thrashing.

What could he have been thinking?
Me! Walk on water? No way!
Then, Peter started to sink.
Down, down, into that fish-laden sea—
the Sea of Galilee.
Peter was a goner or so seemed to be.

Thank God, that's not the end of the story.
You see, Peter *still* had that little mustard seed
clasped tightly in his fist, and Jesus was *still* there
walking on the water.

The Lord reached out His hand.
Up and out the sea Peter came,
like Jonah being spit out the belly of that great fish—
well, you *remember*.

Just where has Peter's mustard seed gone
for lo, these 2000 years or so?
Have you not heard?
It has grown to become a Kingdom of its own
that is now two billion strong.

On its throne sits the Man from Galilee—you *remember*?
The *other* man out on the sea—the One Who,
to this very day—*still* walks on water.

Illumination

The Light of the World

And [Jesus] was transfigured before them: and his face did shine as the sun, and his raiment was white as the light. (Mat 17:2)

* * *

For as the lightning, that lighteneth out of the one part under heaven, shineth unto the other part under heaven; so shall also the Son of man be in his day. (Luk 17:24)

* * *

And the light shineth in darkness; and the darkness comprehended it not. (Joh 1:5)

* * *

For God, who commanded the light to shine out of darkness, hath shined in our hearts, to give the light of the knowledge of the glory of God in the face of Jesus Christ. (2Co 4:6)

What's It All About?

Who shall separate us from the love of Christ? Shall tribulation, or distress, or persecution, or famine, or nakedness, or peril, or sword... For I am persuaded, that neither death, nor life, nor angels, nor principalities, nor powers, nor things present, nor things to come, Nor height, nor depth, nor any other creature, shall be able to separate us from the love of God, which is in Christ Jesus our Lord. (Rom 8:35, 38-39)

The Lord Jesus Christ is that wondrous bright light that shines into every shadow and crevice of our lives, illuminating our purpose and meaning for being here. When it's as dark as it can get, that's when the Lord's light will shine the brightest. For sure, He will always be there for us, revealing the pathway that leads directly to Him.

In our human condition, we have blinders on concerning the spiritual and can only see the short, narrow, dim hallway of our own lives here in the physical. Like the Dionne Warwick classic song "What's It All About, Alfie?," we may sometimes ponder our purpose for being here. We may even wonder like Peggy Lee in another old classic song: "Is This All There Is?" But, as Christians, we don't need to think on these things, for we can have confidence in the Lord to see us through, no matter what. The Bible tells us the Lord sees the whole picture, from beginning to end. Most importantly, He is in control of how it will all turn out, and He has predestined everything to "work together for good" for those who love Him (Rom 8:28).

The Lord is our friend and kinsman when all others have left or betrayed us. He is a parent when our earthly family has passed on or abandoned us, a companion when a spouse is not there, and a counselor to fill an empty void. He is our confidence when we have none. He is our courage when our own fails. He is our strength when the circumstances of life have drained us completely. He is our stamina when we are weak in body, soul, or spirit. He fills us up when we are "running on empty." He is our comfort in a world wracked by pain and suffering.

In Psalm 23, written one thousand years before Jesus visited the earth, we learn through King David how the Lord cares for us. David writes what has now become an old familiar refrain for the Christian: "The Lord is my Shepherd, I shall not want..." Most of us can probably quote the whole psalm by heart. We know, of course, from New Testament Scripture that the "Great Shepherd" in this psalm and the "Good Shepherd" are one and the same. They both are none other than Jesus Christ (Mar 6:34, 14:27; Joh 10:2-17). This alone makes it one of the most powerful and profound passages in the entire Bible.

When we are in Christ, we need not fear being left alone through abandonment, divorce, or widowhood or when physical disease threatens us. We need not fear terrorists, plunderers, or plagues on our country's soil. Of course, that doesn't mean we won't go through trials and hardships. That's part of our flawed human condition. But, when we do, Jesus will be there for us, for He has promised to remain with us in all circumstances. And, in the end, we need not fear even the ultimate destroyer of our physical being. At the very moment of death, the Lord will be there, too. If we have chosen Jesus as our Lord and Savior, He has pledged to carry us to the other side of the "valley" and on into Heaven to be with Him forever.

Benjamin Franklin once wrote that all we can be sure of is "death and taxes." In my old age, however, I've found there's much more to life than that. As Christians, the one great truth is that, through it all, Christ shines brighter than all the celestial lights combined, for He is the "bright and morning star." And, at the end, when the light from the sun, moon, and stars have all gone out, the Lord will still be there illuminating our way. All we need to do is reach out our hand and ask Him to take it. And, when He takes hold of you, dear friend, He will never leave you, forsake you, or let you go. You have His word on it.

And as he [Jesus] prayed, the fashion of his countenance was altered, and his raiment was white and glistering... (Luk 9:29)

These are they which came out of great tribulation, and have washed their robes, and made them white in the blood of the Lamb... (Rev 7:14)

There are times in our lives when the Lord brings us the most spectacular scenes in nature. This poem is about one of those moments. The feelings I had looking out over Lake Sammamish one day at our home in Bellevue, Washington lifted my spirits to the highest levels, and I wanted to praise the Lord with every part of my being. I immediately grabbed my yellow tablet and began jotting down descriptive passages of what I saw, much like a photographer will grab a camera and begin clicking photos. I did not want to lose one part of this beautiful scene that I was so privileged to witness right outside my window.

When I see such glorious beauty in nature, I often wonder how anyone can question the existence of the Creator. How can anyone *not* see a purposeful pattern to this world that could only be conceived and brought into being by a masterful Maker whose abilities are far beyond the comprehension of mere mortals? As for me and my house, we will praise the Lord for all the great things He has done. One of the ways I do this is through my poetry.

To my dear friend, Donna:
We share a love of verse
and lots of good memories.

Some people come into our lives and then quickly depart.
Some stay for a while and leave footprints in our hearts.
—Anon.

Bible Study: Gen 1:1; Psa 2:1-12, 24:1-10, 42:1-2, 72:3, 80:10, 95:4, 121:1-3; Mat 17:5; Joh 1:1-3, 14; Rev 22:1-6.

Metaphor for God

Looking out over the lake, a *whiteness*
even in the absence of snowfall
has wrapped itself around
this bright, spring-like day
that sprouted in the midst of winter.

A linear mist hovers over
sparkling silver waters
in a light, white
gossamer of fog.

Low-lying white blanketed clouds
of ethereal down
settle themselves
on the shoreline.

Cerulean skies are splashed
in a sponge-painted wash of
swirling white, wispy clouds.

As a detached reminder of winter,
white-capped mountains
in the distance beckon
to the season's skiers.

White is the color of winter—
An attribute for purity.
The dress of the Virgin Bride.
The crown on a hoary head.
The background for the writer's ink.
The illumination of angels' wings.
The shroud covering in death.

From the divergent prism of white light,
all colors spring to life.
White is not empirical.
White is spiritual. Ethereal. Divine.
In its purest form, white
is flawless, unblemished perfection.

Looking out over the lake on this day,
I understand why white is a metaphor
for the presence of God.

Tell ye, and bring them near; yea, let them take counsel together: who hath declared this from ancient time? who hath told it from that time? have not I the Lord? and there is no God else beside me; a just God and a Saviour; there is none beside me. (Isa 45:21)

This poem is not about a New Age concept that makes a little "spirit god" out of things in nature like a tree or rock or bear. It's about the Lord God Almighty—Creator of Heaven and Earth. From the pages of the Bible, He tells us: "...there is none beside me" (Isa 45:21). His handiwork can be found everywhere and in everything. Whether we realize it or not and whether we accept it or not, the Lord sees all, hears all, knows all, and is in us all. He is the All-Knowing, Omnipresent, and Omnipotent One True God of the Universe.

The Lord has created a pattern for every inch of the Universe. The evidence of His carefully laid out plans can be found everywhere we look. His handiwork can be seen in the sun, moon, and stars, in the tides, in the changing seasons, and in the movement of the earth as time ticks out the hours of our lives. What is even more amazing is that this magnificent, mighty Creator wants to have a personal, one-on-one relationship with each and every one of us. How awesome is that!

From "Auntie" with love to my nieces, Carrie, Ashleigh, Kelly and their families,
and to my great nephews, Chad and Christian.
And, to my sweet great niece, Ariel, with whom I share a love for
blue jays, hummingbirds, horses, and rock collecting.
You each hold a special place in my heart. Grow strong in the Lord.

Bible Study: Job 38:1-41, 39:1-30; 1Ch 16:30-34; Psa 11:4, 14:2, 34:11, 40:7, 56:8, 78:4, 139:16, 149:2; Isa 29:11-18, 40:28, 43:15-17; Jer 25:13; 1Pe 4:19; Rev 17:8.

The Four Seasons of God

God is in everything and in everywhere we look.
He is with us in every cranny, every crevice, and every nook.
God blows us kisses in the beauty of a rose.
God gives us hugs in the arms of our children as they grow.

God is in the Spring,
in the flowers and in the rain.
He is in the earth's soil when we're planting seeds of grain.
God is in the greenest pastures and in the towering trees.
God is in the sunshine's warmth and in a cooling breeze.

God is in the Summer,
when we're at work or play,
He is in the clearest skies and in the clouds of gray.
God is with us when we labor and when we are at rest.
God is with us always—in our every breath.

God is in the Autumn,
among the amber rust of falling leaves.
He is in the fields of harvest when we're bringing in the sheaves.
God is with us when we're bent down low or when we reach up high.
God is with us everywhere—in earth, wind, sea, and sky.

God is in the Winter,
in the midst of nature's chilling thrust.
He is in the icy seas beneath their frozen crust.
God is there, too, in trees stripped bare of leaves.
God is there in the longest night and in the deepest freeze.

Turn around—look and see.
God is even in the likes of you and in the likes of me.
He is there when conception ignites life's sweet song.
He is there when we make that final sojourn to our eternal home.
God is there holding cradles rocking sweetly in the wind.
God is there destroying empty coffins made of cold, dead sin.

God is in everything and everywhere we look,
for He is the Creator of it all—the author of life's Great Book.
Fall on your knees. Bow your head and pray.
Call on the Lord Jesus now—call on Him today.
As our Maker and the Creator, glorify His name,
for our precious Lord and Savior is One and the Same.

And he shall be as the light of the morning, when the sun rises, even a morning without clouds; as the tender grass springing out of the earth by clear shining after rain. (2Sa 23:4)

I tend to integrate sunrises into my writings quite a bit, for, to me, there is nothing more awe-inspiring in nature than a beautiful sunrise—especially after a rain when the atmosphere is full of ions, making everything brighter and more distinct. Through the years, I've been blessed to have lived in different places where I could wake up and see the sunrise out my window. Such is the case where we live now. One morning, after I had witnessed an extraordinarily gorgeous one, I was reading the Bible and came across the above passage in 2 Samuel. With the sunrise still fresh in my mind, I was especially moved by the powerful, prophetic imagery in this particular verse and the way the writer used a sunrise after a rain to describe the Lord.

The writer of this verse utilized a wealth of familiar Christ symbols, including "light," "morning," "sunrise," and "rain," along with other symbols like "tender grass" to represent people. I could picture in my mind Christians springing up all over the earth like sparkling diamonds after the "clear shining" of God's Word had touched them.

My heart overflowed with praises to the Lord. I quickly sat down at my computer and wrote this poem with the idea of blending together this beautifully descriptive biblical passage with the sunrise I had just seen.

To: Sadie and Jim, Sandy and Fred,
Laurel and Stan, Theo and Jay,
Elaine and Jim, and Verna, Janice,
June, Erika, Lori, and Patty P.
You all sparkle like diamonds.

Nothing but heaven itself is better
than a friend who is really a friend.
—Abraham Lincoln

Bible Study: Gen 1:9-13; Deu 32:1-4; 2Sa 23:1-7; Psa 72:6, 16, 103:13-20, 147:7-8; Isa 40:5-8; Zec 10:1; Mat 6:30; 1Pe 1:24-25; Rev 9:4.

A Clear Shining

The sun rises over the mountain,
its first light bursts forth in blazing splendor,
with a glorious blend of red, purple, and gold,
a true magnificence to behold.

As the light of the morning spreads its full wings,
all traces of dark shadows are erased,
and the cloudless sky ebbs gradually into
a brushed canvas of azure hue.

Blades of tender grass all around
seemingly spring from the ground in rapt attention,
with moist remnants from a recent rain
reflecting tiny dots of morning light
that sparkle bright like diamonds.

The sun has arrived,
and the earth is now alive
with a clear shining.

Inspiration

The Living Word of God

Thy word is a lamp unto my feet, and a light unto my path. (Psa 119:105)

* * *

A word fitly spoken is like apples of gold in pictures of silver. (Pro 25:11)

* * *

Heaven and earth shall pass away, but my words shall not pass away. (Mat 24:35)

Words to the Wise

...And that from a child thou hast known the holy scriptures, which are able to make thee wise unto salvation through faith which is in Christ Jesus. All scripture is given by inspiration of God, and is profitable for doctrine, for reproof, for correction, for instruction in righteousness: That the man of God may be perfect [complete], thoroughly furnished unto all good works. (2Ti 3:15-17)

The Holy Bible is not just any book. It is God's ongoing conversation with us. In one of his sermons, Charles Stanley said: "The Holy Bible is the voice of God in human print." I would add: "...and it never changes." Yes, it is an ancient book, but it will never be an outdated one, for it is timeless. The rules and commandments that applied at the beginning of Genesis—starting with Adam and Eve—still apply to us today and will continue to be relevant in our lives until the end of time and beyond as predicted in Revelation.

The Lord did not just plunk down His faithful ones in the middle of this dark, dangerous world without providing us direction and guidance. To ensure we are properly nurtured and nourished in all areas, we have been given the ultimate reference guide. It is the Holy Bible—God's *Living Word*.

This guide is truly a "multi-functional" work. It does not simply provide a history of God's holy people. Yes, it chronicles their journey as they progressed from the East towards the West. Yet, as an instrument of prophecy, it also sheds light on the *timeline* of our history—past, present, and future. Most important, it provides a *directive* to God's holy people, outlining our collective commission in this world and how we are to go about it.

In its most personal function, the Bible serves as a guide for daily living. Here in the pages of this book, we learn to live according to God's will and not by our own selfish motives, for it was given to teach self-control, restraint, and discipline. It shows us how to draw from the "well" of the Holy Spirit—the One Who dwells within each of us (once we have been saved).

As its most important function, however, the Bible records for all time when, where, how and why God came to earth in the flesh. Thus, throughout history, the Lord has always ensured that His ancient, one-of-a-kind, and supernatural book would survive for one primary reason: It introduces us to *Him*—the One and Only Almighty God of the Universe.

Indeed, the Lord went to a lot of trouble—and many of his prophets died—so we could hold this book in our hands and read it for ourselves. Yes, down through the centuries, it has gone through various translations over many generations. And yet, its timeless messages have remained constant.

Best of all, the Holy Bible tells us how to have an ongoing, personal and up-close relationship with God—in this life and on into Eternity. Indeed, it is not just any book. In fact, it is the *holiest of books*, for it has been supernaturally touched by the hand of Almighty God. This is why it is inerrant—both contextually and spiritually. As such, it is to be held with utmost reverence, respect, and veneration. Let no one tell you differently!

If you want to know God, read the Bible, for it illuminates His multi-faceted relationship with us as Creator. Through the knowledge given in His Word, you can be in communion with Him. The Living Word of God will never let you down. You can depend on it!

...Now go, write it before them in a table, and note it in a book, that it may be for the time to come for ever and ever... (Isa 30:8)

Seek ye out of the book of the Lord, and read: no one of these shall fail, none shall want her mate: for my mouth it hath commanded, and his spirit it hath gathered them... (Isa 34:16)

Then said I, Lo, I come: in the volume of the book it is written of me... (Psa 40:7)

How do you view the Bible when you look at it? Do you see all the enduring, timeless, divine beauty it possesses or do you see an old, outdated book that needs to be discarded or updated to fit our more indulgent, relativistic modern world? Think on this. How you view the Holy Bible can make the difference in how you will spend Eternity.

Bible Study: Gen 5:1; Exo 17:14, 24:7, 32:32-33; Num 21:14; Deu 28:58-61, 30:10, 31:24-26; Jos 1:8, 8:31-34, 18:9, 23:6, 24:26; 1Ki 11:41; 2Ki 22:8-13; Ezr 4:15, 6:18; Neh 8:1-18, 9:3, 12:23, 13:1; Job 19:23, Psa 40:7, 56:8, 139:16; Col 3:12; 1Pe 1:1-3; 2Jo 1:1-2, 1:13.

The Holy Bible

Some can look into her portal eyes
and recognize the finest wine.

Others see only an aged face
with all its lines that's past its prime.

...As it is written, Eye hath not seen, nor ear heard, neither have entered into the heart of man, the things which God hath prepared for them that love him. But God hath revealed them unto us by his Spirit: for the Spirit searcheth all things, yea, the deep things of God...Now we have received, not the spirit of the world, but the spirit which is of God; that we might know the things that are freely given to us of God. (1Co 2:9-10, 12)

...Have they not heard? Yes verily, their sound went into all the earth, and their words unto the ends of the world. (Rom 10:18)

In this fast-paced technological age, the average Christian does not take time to study diligently the precious gift of the Word given to us by God. Instead, most Bible study generally consists of a "patchwork quilt" of supposedly "quality time," with one minute here or five minutes there. Sadly, the majority of our days is spent running after the temporal "tin treasures" of this world. How often do we leave the more valuable "apples of gold," "bowls of silver," and luminous "pearls of wisdom" forsaken in a pile of dust on the bookshelf?

Studying the Scriptures should be an essential facet of our spiritual lives. We are to "eat it" as Paul says until it becomes a part of us. That's how the Word gets into our hearts. Understanding God's Word is not something we can do with a cursory read for five minutes a day. It takes in-depth study and that takes time. Sure, sometimes parts of the Bible may seem boring. For example, who wants to read the Book of Numbers or all the "begets" and "begats?" But, if you continue on, you will receive more blessings than you can ever imagine. Over time, you will be reading with more comprehension. You will find yourself recalling different verses and passages of scripture. This, in turn, can help you relate circumstances in your life to biblical teachings and help resolve personal problems. At times, you may even find the Lord gives you special revelation.

The Bible you hold in the palm of your hand is priceless. Study it. Treasure it. There are an unfathomable amount of "gold nuggets" awaiting you in God's Holy Word—including healing, peace, comfort, forgiveness, wisdom, and hope. The Bible is a most precious gift to be cherished. It is your own personal "love letter" from the Lord. Nowhere can you feel as close to God as when you are reading His Word. Honor it. Keep it close to your heart. Then, always be willing to pass on what you have learned. The Lord will bless you richly when you do.

To Chase, my "buddy," from your Aunt Debbie with love.
You've overcome so much in your young life.
Continue on your journey with the Lord.
He is with you every step of the way.

Bible Study: Gen 8:1, 18:10; Job 28:18; Psa 40:7, 78:39, 102:18, 103:16, 104:3, 139:16, 148:8, 149:9; Pro 30:4; Ecc 12:10; Jer 15:16; Isa 64:1-6, 65:6; Dan 5:24-25, 7:2, 12:1; Zec 2:6; Mal 3:16; Mat 24:14, 31; Mar 13:27, 16:15; Joh 6:31-45, 8:17, 12:16, 15:25, 20:31, 21:25; Act 13:29, 24:14; 1Co 2:9-12; Heb 12:23; 1Pe 1:16; Rev 2:17, 5:1, 14:1, 19:12-16.

Written on the Wind

Can you not hear?
It is written on the Wind.
"Eye has not seen,
nor ear ever heard
the beauty and mystery
found in His Word."[1]

When Christ did come,
He was crucified and died.
But, then He was risen,
and now He is alive!

Today, the Lord's Word has been written
in the hearts of all who follow Him.
Indeed, it has been unfurled,
and the Gospel has now gone throughout the world!

1. Isa 64:4.

And he said, Unto you it is given to know the mysteries of the kingdom of God: but to others in parables; that seeing they might not see, and hearing they might not understand. (Luk 8:10)

In my idealistic youth, I wrote this poem expressing my desire for learning, with the stars representing universal knowledge. I was sixteen and it was one of my first poems. I wasn't aware at the time the answer to the mysteries of the Universe and the "peace of mind" for which I was searching could be found in the worn pages of an old book that lay on my bedside table. It wouldn't be until after years of Bible study that I would realize this fundamental truth.

This might seem like an extraordinary statement, but think about what Jesus said: "Unto you it is given to know the mysteries of the kingdom of God..." That's right. He was speaking to believers—those with the Holy Spirit. And, yes, the Universe is included in God's Kingdom. But, here's "the rub." These "mysteries" have been *hidden* in the Word. The Lord alone reveals them in His own time, only to His holy people, and only that which He deems fit.

Yes, the answers to all the unfathomable questions in the Universe can be found in this Holy Book. Yet, the vast majority of these mysteries will remain hidden until Jesus returns. In the end, He will reveal how everything was ordered and written down ahead of time in His Word. In the meantime, the Lord simply doesn't want this information falling into the hands of the enemy.

Sadly, for the most part, mankind uses knowledge for evil and not for good. This is why no person or group can ever have the complete knowledge of all spiritual mysteries while the world remains in its imperfect state. For now, the Holy Bible will remain God's witness and record of the truth—the reality of Who Jesus is and the meaning of it all. We, as Christians, accept this on faith.

Yes, there on that bedside table had been the "star" I was looking for in my youth. Within the pages of the Holy Bible are the answers to the mysteries of the Universe, including its origin, the identity of its Creator, where we come from, and where we are going. This "light" is a gift we can all hold in the palm of our hands. In return, we are to study the Word regularly and show ourselves "approved unto God" so we are able to "rightly divide the word of truth" (2Ti 2:15).

For these reasons, this poem holds a very important place for me in this collection. When searching for truth, it is a reminder not to look in all the wrong places. There is only *one* source that can be trusted, and that is God's Holy Word. The key to unlocking that Word is Jesus. We can trust Him to reveal information to us "as needed" in order to fulfill His purposes rather than our own. After all, the Lord is All-Knowing, Omnipotent, Omnipresent, and Almighty. He is God, Creator of the Universe. When we get to Heaven, we'll have an eternity for all these mysteries to be unveiled. I can wait until then.

Bible Study: Gen 1:1, 32:10; Isa 9:2, 6-7; Dan 2:23, 10:5-8, 21; Zec 4:6; Mat 16:19; Luk 8:10; Joh 16:12-14; Act 9:5, 26:14; 1Co 13:12; 2Ti 2:15; 1Pe 2:9-10.

The Great Riddle

The stars come out slowly,
one at a time.
I wish I could catch one
and say it were mine.

I wish I could hold it
in the palm of my hand.
I wish I could examine
this mystery to man.

I could then say to the world,
I've solved your great riddle.
The problem was simple, easy,
and little.

But of all else that I might find,
to me most important
would be peace of mind.

Proclamation

Who Is This Man Called Jesus?

And it shall be said in that day, Lo, this is our God; we have waited for him, and he will save us: this is the Lord; we have waited for him, we will be glad and rejoice in his salvation. (Isa 25:9)

* * *

And I saw heaven opened, and behold a white horse; and he that sat upon him was called Faithful and True...And the armies which were in heaven followed him upon white horses, clothed in fine linen, white and clean...And I saw a great white throne, and him that sat on it, from whose face the earth and the heaven fled away... (Rev 19:11, 14, 20:11)

My God

Jesus Christ the same yesterday, and to day, and for ever. (Heb 13:8)

My God is not whatever I think Him to be, for He is far beyond the comprehension of man. He is not whatever I want Him to be, for He *made* me—I didn't create Him. I was not born with a little god already within me nor will I grow into a god through a series of reincarnated lives. No, *My God* comes to dwell within me in the here and now through my *spirit*. That said, He is not an intrusive or controlling God—for only if I ask will He abide with me and direct my path.

My God is not contained in a box, relying on the legalistic rhetoric of a chosen, select few. Neither is *My God* a distant, cold, dispassionate "being" who remains out of reach and out of touch. No indeed! *My God* has an upfront and personal relationship with me, for He is my best friend. Even though He will not always release me from bad circumstances, He has promised to see me through—no matter what!

My God accepts me just as I am—with all my faults and foibles. *My God* loves me unconditionally, sets me free from the bonds of this world, and saves my soul for eternity—redeeming me through the grace of His tender mercies. *My God* does not coerce me or shackle me or force me to serve Him. *My God* loves me so much that He has given me free will. It is therefore up to me whether or not I follow Him.

My God doesn't show favoritism for one group over another or from one person to another. I do not have to be of a certain race or nationality nor do I have to attain more knowledge than someone else. *My God* takes me just the way I am. *My God* does not require me to follow prescribed rituals as proof of my good faith nor am I required to work for my salvation or status in heaven. *My God* does not require me to harm others for any reason. Matter of fact, He expects me to do *good* to those who would do evil to me.

My God does not require me to go on pilgrimages or to search for Him in far-off places, for He is always with me. I do not need to possess a special intellect nor do I need to retain a favored status through birth. In fact, there is nothing I can do to earn His grace, for it is a free gift. *My God* looks only at the condition of my heart and my willingness to accept Him on faith, to love Him, and to follow Him.

Who is *My God* that requires so little and yet gives so much? He is the Creator of the Universe and everything in it—from the microscopic molecules that form the basis of all life to the vast, glorious intergalactic cosmos with its splendid array of stars and planets. *My God* wrote the Master Plan for this Universe, and He expects me to accept that Plan on faith while abiding by the principles and precepts of His Word.

My God has many different names. He is Wonderful, Counselor, and Almighty Father. He is the Great I Am, the Word, the Great Shepherd, the Lamb, Immanuel, Jehovah Jireh, Yahweh, Alpha and Omega, the Beginning and the End, the Root and Offspring of David, the Bright and Morning Star, the Lion of Judah, and King of the Universe. Yes, He is all that and more. As the Second Personage of the Holy Trinity, He is *all* and is in us all.

You see, *My God* is my Lord and personal Savior, Jesus Christ of Nazareth. As God the Son, He loved me so much that He emptied Himself of the Godhead, came down from Heaven to earth, and was conceived of the Holy Spirit in the form of a man. He was born of a Virgin, lived a perfect, sinless life, was crucified, and died for the sins of the world. Then, He was resurrected and is now sitting at the right hand of the Father in Heaven. He will return one day in victory and glory so all who believe in Him can live for eternity in peace and harmony and love.

Why would *My God* do all that? Because He loves me! And, He loves *you*, too. He loves all His children so much that, through His sacrifice on the Cross at Calvary, He gave everyone on this planet—past, present, and future—the choice either to accept Him or reject Him.

Yes, that's why *My God* died on the Cross, and that's why He rose again, and that's why He will come again. You see, He will return one day so that each and everyone on this earth who has chosen to follow Him by faith will receive eternal salvation and will abide with Him in Heaven forever and ever. *My God! He is magnificent!*

Holy! Holy! Holy! In the name of God the Father, God the Son, and God the Holy Spirit—One God in Three Persons—Blessed Trinity.

Upon the four and twentieth day of the eleventh month, which is the month Sebat...I saw by night, and behold a man riding upon a red horse, and he stood among the myrtle trees that were in the bottom; and behind him were there red horses, speckled, and white...And the man that stood among the myrtle trees answered and said, These are they whom the Lord hath sent to walk to and fro through the earth... (Zec 1:7-10)

Among theologians, it is fairly well accepted that the "man among the myrtles trees" in Chapter One of the Book of Zechariah is Jesus Christ and His "red" (chestnut) horse represents His blood sacrifice and "First Coming." It's just one of the many "snapshots" of the Messiah we are given throughout the Old Testament.

Further on in Chapter Six, Zechariah tells us these beautiful horses that were with the Lord among the myrtle trees represent the "four spirits of heaven." They are prophetic conveyances propelled and guided by the wondrous workings of the Holy Spirit. The ones going North, Zechariah tells us, bring "rest" to the earth, for they have "quieted the Lord's spirit." In a future time, he is told, the horses and their chariots will be going "to and fro throughout the earth" dispensing spiritual rest and peace.

Now, fast forward to after Christ was resurrected. This "rest and peace" that Zechariah prophesied is found in the Resurrected Christ. The writer tells us in Hebrews: "There remaineth therefore a rest to the people of God" (Heb 4:9). This "rest" we have now entered into through Christ comes from the indwelling of God the Holy Spirit.

This vivid imagery in Zechariah of the Holy Spirit going throughout the earth is also reminiscent of the passage in the New Testament where Jesus tells His disciples: "...the Comforter, which is the Holy Ghost, whom the Father will send in my name, he shall teach you all things, and bring all things to your remembrance, whatsoever I have said unto you" (Joh 14: 26). As Christians, we are to follow the Holy Spirit on the path to "rest and peace" found in Christ as others have done down through the ages since Jesus walked the earth. This we do through the study of His Word and with fervent prayer. It is our *biblical quest*. The Good News is, when Christ returns, all His followers will be taken out before the Lord's judgment comes down. Then, we will have the honor of "following" behind Him as He rides to victory on His "white horse" (Rev 19:11).

If you haven't already, will you ask the Lord into your heart? Join us while you can on this glorious quest—while the "heavenly horses" of the Holy Spirit are still pointing the way toward Heaven.

> To my two wonderful sons, Charles and Christopher.
> Continue to be confident and strong in your faith.
> It is a joy journeying together on our biblical quest.
> From Mom with love.

Bible Study: Job 9:1-14; Jos 24:6-7; Isa 2:7, 5:28, 21:1-12, 30:16, 31:3, 66:20; Jer 4:13, 8:16, 12:5, 17:25, 46:4, 47:3; Eze 39:20; Amo 5:1-27, 6:12; Nah 3:2; Hab 3:8; Zec 1:7-11, 4:2, 6:1-8, 14:20; Luk 11:2; Joh 14:16, 15:26, 16:7; Jam 3:3; Rev 1:16, 6:1-11, 9:9, 19:4.

Follow the Horses: The Quest

From the pages of the Ancient One
come Zechariah's horses in full gallop, [1]
speeding on glistening, sinewy thigh,
in poetic patterns across the sky
to deliver messages of eternal consequence.

Panting, snorting, without warning,
their indelible, inevitable prophecies will arrive.
In them we can see all the Western horses of perpetuity.
Great stallions of nobility.
The workhorse of stability.
The circus horse of versatility.
The thoroughbred of agility.
The war horse of mobility.

As the horses pause with their Master
to rest at ease among the myrtle trees,
a dove takes flight in the night sky.
In earnestness I listen to His Word.
I hear a bough break and the Cradle falls.
"How long?" I ask aloud in wonderment and awe.

He turns and speaks, a riddle forms:
"If you will ask, then ask. I will return. Now come, [2]
for it will be done on earth as it is in Heaven. [3]
Take your leave, if you will, and follow the horses."
So, off I go again into a sea of visionary dreams.

As they gallop throughout the corridors of time,
I follow these ethereal steeds in their race,
keeping pace with history—
over rivers, plains, and mountain ranges,
through darkened forests and shadowed valleys,
past lavish palaces and civilized savages.

Suddenly, the gallant beasts running four abreast,
divide among the stars, going North, South, East, and West,
in a synchronized array of black, white, red, and speckled gray,
hastening on towards Destiny.

Then, I remember again the words of the Man at ease in the myrtle trees,
and follow the horses going North toward the Pleiades—
heading straight on into the Morning.

1. Zec 6:1-8; 2. Isa 21:12; 3. Luk 11:2.

For God so loved the world that he gave his only begotten son... (Joh 3:16) ...That was the true Light, which lighteth every man that cometh into the world... (Joh 1:9) ...Blessed are all they that put their trust in him... (Psa 2:12) ...Father, forgive them for they know not what they do... (Luk 23:34) ...The Lord is my Shepherd, I shall not want... (Psa 23:1) ...Jesus said: I am the good shepherd: the good shepherd giveth his life for the sheep... (Joh 10:11) ...He was in the world, and the world was made by him, and the world knew him not. He came unto his own, and his own received him not... (Joh 1:10-11) ...Lift up your heads, O ye gates; and be ye lifted up, ye everlasting doors; and the King of glory shall come in...Who is this King of glory? The LORD of hosts, he is the King of glory. (Psa 24:7-8, 10)

As we study the Bible, we see that Jesus was the Messiah prophesied long ago to come into this world as God in the flesh. Yes, it was made known ahead of time. He would come as the Sacrificial Lamb to provide grace and salvation to a lost and dying people. He would come as a Shepherd calling His lost sheep home. And, He will return again as the King in all His glory to take His children with Him to Heaven.

These different roles of the Messiah were prophesied in many Old Testament passages. Several of these prophecies are found in the Psalms, but the three specific ones mentioned above really stand out. In Psalm 22, the Messiah is the "Suffering Servant." This psalm is a depiction of Jesus on the Cross written 1000 years before it actually happened and centuries before crucifixion even became a form of execution. In Psalm 23, the Messiah is the "Great Shepherd," i.e. the "Good Shepherd." In the Book of John, Chapter 10, Jesus says He is "the Good Shepherd." Then, in Psalm 24, we find the Messiah depicted at the Second Coming as the "King" in all His glory, returning to redeem those who have accepted Him.

Jesus *the Christ*—our Messiah—offers salvation, grace, and eternal life to a dying world. Why would anyone reject such a magnanimous offer from the Creator of it all? Why would one even pause to ponder the credibility of such a noble gesture? Why would anyone ever doubt the authenticity of this selfless act that is so well documented in both Old and New Testament texts? Instead, why not simply accept this beautiful, bountiful gift that was presented to each and every one of us at such great sacrifice?

Why not ask Jesus into your heart this very day? You have an eternity to gain—and nothing to lose!

To my friends and fellow Christian writers, Steve and "Sis" Patty:
Thank you for your support and encouragement
to keep me writing verse. It has meant so much to me.

*What draws people to be friends is that they see
the same truth. They share it.*
—C.S. Lewis

Bible Study: Gen 3:15, 49:10; Psa 22, 23, 24; Ecc 12; Isa 6:1-8, 9:1-8, 40:3-18, 53:1-12; Mat 3:15-17, 17:5; Mar 1:11; Joh 10:11-16; 2Pe 1:17; Jde 1:25; Rev 4:8, 22:6-16.

Who is the Christ?

Who is the Christ, the Messiah?
He is the Second Person of the Trinity.
He has been alive for Infinity.
He is the Creator of the Universe
Who made us in His image.

He is Jesus Christ of Nazareth.
God in the flesh before us.
He has come from Heaven to set us free
and to take us with Him into Eternity.
For this, He will always and forever be
our Lord, our God, our Savior, our King.

For we have not followed cunningly devised fables, when we made known unto you the power and coming of our Lord Jesus Christ, but were eyewitnesses of his majesty...when there came such a voice to him from the excellent glory, This is my beloved Son, in whom I am well pleased...We have also a more sure word of prophecy; whereunto ye do well that ye take heed, as unto a light that shines in a dark place, until the day dawn, and the day star arise in your hearts... (2Pe 1:16-19)

Just as the world knows the sun will come up every morning, Christians have the blessed assurance that Jesus Christ will return one day for us, His children. Jesus said it, and we can believe it. The time of His Second Coming was established before the beginning of this world. He is our Day Star rising.

With love to: Gene and Mylo.
Cortney and Amy, Paige, Ryan, and Jessica.
Natalie, Gordy, and Kendall Grace.
Alex and Monet.

Come join us in the *Son*-rise!

Bible Study: Gen 1:1-3; Psa 19:7-9, 119:105; Pro 6:23; Isa 8:20, 9:2, 50:10, 60:1-2; Mat 4:16; Luk 1:78-79; Joh 1:7-9, 5:35-39, 8:12; 2Co 4:4-6; 1Pe 1:10; 2Pe 1:16-21; Rev 2:28, 22:16.

Day Star Rising

Just before Morning bathes the world
in an incandescent splendor,
and before Darkness has totally passed,
the eastern horizon is illuminated in a fiery blaze.
It is the Day Star rising.

With every corner and crevice of this world
awakened from the Night,
all eyes of Creation focus on its Light.
The glorious warmth and beauty of the Earth
is reborn once again.

In ancient ages of eons past,
this dawning hour was set with a sure Word.
Thus, with a certainty, we can know
the Day Star will appear on time,
rising out of Darkness to shine
on a world lost and stumbling in an empty,
endless void of its own deviant machinations.

In a vacuous valley of blackest shadows,
we faithfully wait for its return,
lifting our voices in a quiet, spiritual refrain,
while we remain vigilant and sustained.

Yes, without a doubt, we know—
even when the deepest depths of Darkness overflow.
It's on its way. It's coming.
Soon, it will arrive. Can't you see its Light?
The Day Star is rising.

Redemption

Jesus Saves

As it is written, There is none righteous, no, not one: There is none that understandeth, there is none that seeketh after God. They are all gone out of the way, they are together become unprofitable; there is none that doeth good, no, not one...But now the righteousness of God without the law is manifested, being witnessed by the law and the prophets; Even the righteousness of God which is by faith of Jesus Christ unto all and upon all them that believe: for there is no difference: For all have sinned, and come short of the glory of God... (Rom 3:10-12, 21-23)

Louis Zamperini: The Heart of a Hero

I will say of the LORD, He is my refuge and my fortress: my God; in him will I trust. (Psa 91:2)

Many have seen the movie, *Unbroken*, about the American war hero, Louis Zamperini. If any person ever went through "deserts" in his life, this man most certainly did. A world-class Olympic track star and World War II hero, Zamperini's heart-wrenching story is chronicled in this excellent film. As a young man, he survived two plane crashes, a record-breaking 47 days adrift at sea, and two years as a prisoner in a Japanese POW camp where he was tortured daily by a cruel prison guard nicknamed "The Bird," a man who was bent on breaking his spirit. Based on the book by Laura Hillenbrand, the movie, however, omits the last crucial chapters of the story. These include Mr. Zamperini's conversion to Christianity after the war and the marvelous transformation that finding Christ made in his life.

After the perils and torture he had experienced during the war, Louis was left hopeless and angry. Unable to cope with his feelings, his life back home in the States fell apart, and he found himself in a deep, dark pit of depression and alcoholism. His wife, in a last-ditch effort to save their marriage, took her reluctant husband to a Billy Graham "tent crusade." The first time he heard the Reverend speak, Zamperini literally ran out, not wanting to accept any of it. But, miraculously, he returned the next night. It was then that he encountered Christ's life-altering power and gave his heart to the Lord.

About that night, Zamperini said: "I knew I was through getting drunk, I knew I was through smoking, and I knew I'd forgiven all of my guards including 'The Bird.' Never dawned on me again that I hated the guy. That was the first night in all those years I'd never had a nightmare, and I haven't had one since." He summed it up by saying: "The heart of this story is when I found Christ as my Savior. That's the heart of my whole life." [1]

Before we saw this movie, my husband had already read the book. He was so impressed he began reading different sections to me. At times, we both found ourselves in tears over the trials and tribulations this poor man endured at the hands of the enemy. But, it was what happened to him *after* the war that was even more phenomenal. He could have said: "Is this all there is?" and continued in mental anguish for the rest of his life.

Instead, Mr. Zamperini chose Christ, and that made all the difference. He went on to become a Christian motivational speaker and dedicated his life to helping young people. He even made two trips to Japan and spoke with some of his old prison guards, telling them he had forgiven them. The guard known as "The Bird," however, refused to meet with him.

Zamperini died at age 97 having lived a glorious, purpose-filled life for Christ that inspired millions of people around the world. Yes, Christ does make all the difference! You can depend on Him to carry you through any and all circumstances. The life of Louis Zamperini is a testament to this truth.

1. Quote from *Captured By Grace*, Billy Graham Evangelistic Association.

To all our American veterans and men and women in uniform, thank you for your service! Also, a special salute to family and friends who have served, including:

- My husband, Chuck Adams (USAF/9th AF Band)
- My late father, Sgt. David Franklin Bullard (US Army/Career/WWII)
- My brothers, Maj. Stanley Bullard (USAF/Career/Vietnam War) and David Bullard (US Army/Germany)
- My late brother-in-law, Lt. Robert J. Salvesen (US Navy/WWII)
- My niece, Col. Jean Arnold (Texas Army National Guard & US Army/Career/Iraq & Afghanistan)
- My nephews, David Keel (Louisiana National Guard/Career/Bosnia, Persian Gulf War, Iraq, & Afghanistan) and Jim Anderson (US Navy)
- Our friends Ian MacRobbie (USAF/9th AF Band), Doug Waddell (US Army/Vietnam), Noah Sherrill (US Army/Afghanistan), Jim Hartman (US Army), and Ray Richard (U.S. Army Special Forces/Vietnam)

Therefore said he [Jesus] unto them, The harvest truly is great, but the labourers are few: pray ye therefore the Lord of the harvest, that he would send forth labourers into his harvest. (Luk 10:2)

In Luke, Chapter 10 we read that Jesus sent out His first "recruits" to bring in believers for God's new Kingdom. He was testing these new disciples to see how they would fare, much like fresh Army recruits on their first mission. He made sure they were prepared spiritually. At the same time, however, Jesus commanded them not to take any essentials that would normally be needed for such a journey. Instead, they had to step out on faith, believing their physical needs would be met. These disciples were to depend upon the kindness of strangers. In the end, the mission was successful, for Luke tells us: "Seventy went out and seventy returned."

Today, as Christians, each of us has a responsibility to "recruit" new believers into the Kingdom. Even so, we aren't all intended to be preachers, evangelists, or missionaries. Still, we can do our part to answer the call of Christ right here in our own little corner of the world. As we go about our daily lives in the will of God and reach out to other people, we are doing God's work. When we are faithful in obeying Christ, like the seventy that Jesus sent out as His first "recruits," we will be successful in "bringing in the laborers" for the Kingdom.

To Noah and his family, good friends and strong Christians.

Once the feet are put right, all the rest of him will follow.
—C.S. Lewis, *The Lion, the Witch, and the Wardrobe*

Bible Study: Ex 23:16; Psa 147:4; Isa 18:4-5, 40:26, 42:1; Jer 5:24, 51:33; Hos 6:11; Joe 3:13; Mat 9:37-38, 24:24; Mar 13:20-27; Luk 10:1-42; Joh 14:2-3; Rom 9:11, 11:5-7; Col 3:12; 2Ti 2:10; Tit 1:1; 1Pe 1:2, 5:13; 2Pe 1:10.

Lord of the Harvest

Lambs among the wolves.
Wheat and chaff growing together in the field.
Harmless doves amid venomous vipers.
Evil abounds. God's word resounds.
It is the End *and* the Beginning.

Power is given the footmen to tread the serpent.
Subjection is a potent medication.
Seventy went out. Seventy returned.
The sick are healed. The lame walk.
The deaf hear. The blind see.
Scorpions flee. Slaves are set free.

Jesus said: *"Rejoice in Me, for your name is written in the heavens."*

Ears have not heard. Eyes have not seen.
Such mysteries are not given to
either the prophet or the king.

Jesus said: *"Were it not so, I would have told you."*

Peter and John re-stated. Paul later reiterated.
Stephen would say it, too.
Bleak is not the message.
White is the driven snow.
Did you not know how the Samaritan went down to Jericho?

Jesus said: *"The Father is to the Son as the Son is to the Father."*

Answer right and live forever.
What is written in the Law?
Do you not comprehend?
Chorazin and Tyre?
Bethsaida and Sidon?
Samaria and Capernaum?
Babylon and Jerusalem?

Jesus said: *"The stars appear one by one. I have named them with my tongue. And, on the morrow, I will come."*

Who are the elect?
They are the ones who love the Lord with all that is within them—
heart, soul, strength, and mind.
Those who choose the "Good" and discard the "Evil."
Those who repay "mean" with "kind."
Above all, they remember forever the Bread and the Wine.
The elect worship the One Who Lives—the Lord of the Harvest.

Jesus saith unto him, I am the way, the truth, and the life: no man cometh unto the Father, but by me. (Joh 14:6)

"I am," Jesus begins this most beautiful poetic verse of Scripture. These two words echo down from the ancient pages of the Holy Book proclaimed time and again in the Old Testament by the great God Jehovah of the Hebrew nation—Who He is, was, and forever will be.

Your understanding and acceptance of this succinct statement determines the very state of your eternal soul. In this one verse, Jesus reveals the only way to Heaven for each and every one of us. There has never been nor will there ever be any individual like the one called Jesus Christ of Nazareth who walked the earth 2000+ years ago. He is God in the flesh come down from Heaven to save mankind.

When the Lord walked the earth, He was the fulfillment of the Old Testament prophecies regarding the Messiah (see Luk 4:16-21). And yet, His disciples did not fully comprehend the complexity of it all until *after* He died on the Cross and was resurrected. Still, they had faith in Him as their Messiah and followed Him, pledging their hearts and their lives. Later, they would spread this great truth throughout the Roman world.

After the Resurrection, the Apostles continued to teach there is no other path to Heaven except through the saving grace of Jesus Christ. Later, the Apostle Paul would go to great lengths in his writings to underscore and explain this in the simplest terms. In fact, he made it quite plain: We can't get there through bloodlines, good works, financial payments, or through some secret "back door." Jesus is our only "ticket" into Heaven.

Our God, the Creator of all the Universe, was willing to become a man, live a humble, mortal existence, and to die a terrible, horrible death on the Cross to ensure that all who would hear His voice and accept the reality of Who He is would live forever with Him in Heaven. So it is written, and so we wait expectantly for His return.

To my beloved husband, Chuck:
You have always been there for me.
This is your favorite Bible verse. It says so much.

Bible Study: Gen 1 & 2; Exo 32:33; Job 9 & 38; Psa 40:7, 10, 43:3, 69:28, 78:21-22, 89:14, 139:7-14; Isa 30:8; Amo 5:8; Zec 14:9; Mal 3:16; Mat 1:1, 4:12-17, 12:15-21, 24:30, 26:24, 61-64; Mar 1:5, 9:23, 11:23, 14:21-28, 16:16; Joh 1:1-5, 14, 23, 3:15-18, 6:47, 8:24, 11:25, 12:12-16, 14:1, 20:31; Act 13:33; Rom 1:17, 3:10, 8:36, 9:33, 14:33, 15:9; Php 4:3; 1Co 2:9; 1Th 4:13-14; 5:3; Heb 10:7; Rev 3:15, 5:1-9, 10:3-4, 17:8, 20:12-15.

As It Is Written

Our Lord Jesus Christ is the God of *Everything*.
He formed the foundation of all creation.
He set the stars in their places.
He fashioned man in multi-colored races.
He made the earth, moon and sun, and when it was all done,
He rested in the cool of the evening, nestled in Eden's wood,
proclaiming all was "Good."

Who says God does not care or that He isn't even there?
In reality, He resides and abides everywhere!
North, South, East, and West. Up, down, and all around.
Beneath the seas and among the stars.
From Orion to Jupiter—from the Milky Way to Mars.

As the Creator of all the earth and the Universe besides,
at the time of His choosing, the Lord will ride,
with His double-edged sword held high,
in chariots of fire across the sky.

With a host of angels following close behind,
in one magnificent moment of time,
He will come to earth in a blaze of glory,
fulfilling that wonderful, familiar old story.

It is then, in all His abounding Grace,
the whole world will meet Him face to face.
As He steps down on hallowed ground,
all the peoples of the earth will bow down.
It is in that moment of great wonder,
our Lord in a voice of Seven Thunders,
will divide the globe asunder.

At the last, He will open the Book, and when it is read,
He will judge both the living and the dead.
And when all is said that is to be said,
those who rejected Him will be rejected,
and those who accepted Him will be accepted.

As Christians, we knew from the beginning this was to be expected.
The world could not go on without being corrected.
All this is found in His Holy Word.
Through it the truth is heard—the truth of the Living God.

> *As it is written, so it was.*
> *As it is written, so it shall be.*
> *As it is written, so it is done.*

Blessed be the God and Father of our Lord Jesus Christ, which according to his abundant mercy hath begotten us again unto a lively hope by the resurrection of Jesus Christ from the dead, to an inheritance incorruptible, and undefiled, and that fadeth not away, reserved in heaven for you, who are kept by the power of God through faith unto salvation ready to be revealed in the last time. (1Pe 1:3-5)

After I studied this passage written by the Apostle Peter, my heart jumped at all the possible meanings of his phrase, "a lively hope." I looked up the synonyms for "lively." These included "animated," "vigorous," "spirited," "sparkling," and "dynamic." I then added another word to that list—"dancing." The hope we have in Christ literally "dances" in our hearts. It's a dazzling, animated hope that lights up our spirits like sparklers on the Fourth of July.

The love Peter had for our Savior passionately pours from the written pages of his epistle. This "lively" hope in Jesus that Peter speaks about is tied to Christ's promise regarding our immortality and eternal life. He goes on to say our inheritance given by Christ will never "fade away" and that it remains "reserved," ready, and waiting for every believer to claim. You could say it has an eternal "life-time guarantee."

Indeed, when we believe in Christ and accept Him as our Savior, we will live with Him forever.

To all my cousins and their families: I love you each and every one.
To Frances and Ed, Shirley and Jimmy, Margaret, Patsy, Becky, Claudette,
Pat, Marygail, Gene, Terry, and to Nadine, Fay, Cheryl, Victor, and Kay,
as well as to Aunt Louise and to Annie Ruth, a dear family friend.

And, always in our hearts are those who have passed on to be with
the Lord: Mama and Daddy, Uncle Elmer and Aunt Mag, Aunt Evelyn
and Uncle Abie, Uncle Ellis and Aunt Mary, Estine and Charlie Medlin,
Uncle Worth, Rhett Cooper, and Catherine Cooper, as well as cousins
Barbara, Abie Jr., Spencer, Jimmy K., and Jimmy Clark and Jerry Douglas.
They are gone, but not forgotten.

...thou, O LORD, shall endure for ever; and thy
remembrance unto all generations. (Psa 103:12)

Bible Study: Psa 22, 23, 24; Isa 9:6-7, 55:1, 6-11; 1Co 15:51-54; 1Pe 1:3-5; 2Pe 3:9; Jde 1:20-25; Rev 22.

A Lively Hope

This old world is simply a transitory dream
that will soon fade from the physical into the spiritual,
with the souls of the saved passing from
the corruptible form of the temporal into
the incorruptible form of the Heavenly—
from the mortal into Immortality,
residing forever in the everlasting, glorious Realm
that is the Throne of God.

This is the wondrous "lively hope"
that is given us when we come on faith,
believing in and accepting
the life, the resurrection, and the glory
that is Jesus Christ our Lord.

Affirmation

Confess With Your Mouth That Jesus Is Lord

But what saith it? The word is nigh thee, even in thy mouth, and in thy heart: that is, the word of faith, which we preach; That if thou shalt confess with thy mouth the Lord Jesus, and shalt believe in thine heart that God hath raised him from the dead, thou shalt be saved.

For with the heart man believeth unto righteousness; and with the mouth confession is made unto salvation. For the scripture saith, Whosoever believeth on him shall not be ashamed... For whosoever shall call upon the name of the Lord shall be saved...So then faith cometh by hearing, and hearing by the word of God. (Rom 10: 8-13, 17)

Sunrise on the Mountain

From the rising of the sun unto the going down of the same the LORD'S name is to be praised. (Psa 113:3)

A new Christian recently asked me what to do when the "new" wears off her faith. It made me think. In all my years of being a Christian, the "new" has never worn off for me. But, there are days when I feel down. When I do, I go to the Word and spend extra time in Bible study.

The Scriptures are like a beautiful sunrise that is different every day. Each morning, when I look upon those holy pages the words are fresh and new. They are like sunbeams warming the soul. That said, we can all expect to have days when there is a lingering "fog" over our minds and spirits. When this happens, we just can't see the "Son" clearly.

We recently moved from the city to the country. We're still trying to decide whether we live on a "big hill" or a "little mountain." Regardless, up high like this, on a clear day we can see the sunrise in all its splendor. Living in a rainy climate, however, there can be days and sometimes weeks when we're "socked in" with complete cloud cover. I call these "dreary, drizzle days." From October through March, there is a continual veil of misty fog and rain. During that time, we're lucky if the sun peeks out for a couple of minutes in the course of the day.

I'm not complaining, mind you. It's the rain that gives us our majestic fir trees and beautiful green landscape. My point here is that every day the sun comes up, but sometimes we can't see it because of cloud cover. That doesn't mean it isn't there. Even through the clouds and rain, we can still see its light. But, it's those special clear days that make all the difference. When we do see the sunrise in all its glory, it is magnificent!

The irony here is that, in the summertime, we often see the sunrise every single day. When that happens, it begins to lose its special appeal. The sunrise has its biggest impact when we haven't seen it in a while. Then, if it's one of those spectacular times where the sky is all lit up in purples and corals and gold—oh, my! It can take your breath away.

It can be the same with the Bible. If you read it every day it can become all too familiar. As you continue reading the same things over and over, you might find yourself lost in a "brain fog"— much like those "dreary, drizzle days" when there's too much cloud cover. Then, one day, something's different. You open the book, and the deepest meaning of the words literally jumps out at you. The Lord has opened your eyes to something you've never seen before.

For a moment in time, He has given you a special revelation. I like to call it "an epiphany." Just like when the clouds clear and you can see the sunrise, the words in a passage that you have read over and over again can suddenly pierce the "cloud cover of your mind." When this happens, the Lord's magnificent light shines through. At such a moment, it can literally take your breath away—just like that glorious sunrise.

So, if you find yourself lost in one of those "dreary, drizzle days" and want to give up on your daily Bible reading, don't. Keep reading the Word. That spectacular "*Son*-rise" is coming. Just wait and see!

To our neighbors and friends on the mountain:
Ray and Jeane
Bob and Lorraine
Tim, Kim, and Kayla
And to our "water treatment guy" and friend, C.J.

And being found in fashion as a man, he [Jesus] humbled himself, and became obedient unto death, even the death of the cross... For the preaching of the cross is to them that perish foolishness; but unto us which are saved it is the power of God. (Php 2:8; 1Co 1:18)

This poem is based on Luke, Chapter 11. It is here in these pages that Jesus demonstrates how to pray through what is known as "The Lord's Prayer." It is here He teaches the Disciples about giving, about forgiveness—not only forgiving others, but also asking for forgiveness—and how simple it is to be received by Him. In my poem, I touch on only a few of the "jewels" found in this chapter, but there is so much more here. It is ideal for in-depth study.

Jesus also hints at dangers the Disciples will face from the religious leaders of their day. He knew well what religious factions had done to His holy prophets through the centuries and what they were planning for Him. Though the Disciples did not yet know it, Jesus was preparing them for what was to come.

For centuries before Christ came to earth, He called forth His prophets in the Scriptures of the Old Testament to proclaim His coming. His voice has resonated throughout time to announce that He, the One that "was, and is, and is to come," (Rev 1:8) would be born a mortal man into a world that would reject Him, crucify Him, and hang Him on a cross to die. Despite all this, while Christ was here, He would bring healings and miracles like the world had never seen.

From the sacrifice of this one man from Heaven would come almighty power to cleanse us from all unrighteousness and save our souls for Eternity. In the end, there would be *one* symbol that pointed to His purpose and reason for coming to earth—the Cross at Calvary.

Still, the significance of that symbol would not be made known to Christ's followers until much later. It would not be at the moment when He was nailed to the Cross. It would not be while he was hanging there. It would not even be when He died. No, it was not until *after* Christ was resurrected from the grave—when He visited His disciples in the Spirit. Only then would they truly know it was *God* Who had hung on that Cross. It was *God* Who had died for the sins of all mankind so that those Who would accept Him would have life and "life...more abundantly," both in this world and in the world to come (Joh 10:10).

Jesus was God in the flesh come in the form of a humble carpenter. How do we know this is true? We know because He lives! Yes, Jesus of Nazareth *is* the Christ, the Messiah—God the Son—come from Heaven to save us, and the only sign given is the Cross. Christ's followers were given this magnificent truth, and they would eventually go on to tell all who would listen. Thus, the Kingdom of God would continue to grow through the centuries.

To: Bill & Rhonda, Antoinette & Jon, Brandon, and Eli.
Good food, pleasant conversation,
and strong Christian camaraderie.
What can be better than that!
From Aunt Debbie with love!

Bible Study: 1Ch 29:11; Mat 6:9-13, 10:38, 16:24; Mar 8:34, 10:21; Luk 9:23, 11:1-13, 14:27; Joh 10:9-18, 19:17-19; 1Co 1:17-18; Gal 6:14; Eph 2:16; Php 2:8; Col 1:4-29, 2:13-15.

The Only Sign Given

Lord, teach us to pray. Tell us what to say.

Our Father, Who art in heaven, Hallowed be thy name.
Thy kingdom come... [1]

The finger of God has pointed.
The dumb speak. Devils are thrown out.
Beelzebub is overcome.
The Kingdom of God is upon you.

...Thy will be done on earth as it is in heaven... [1]

Your friend's friend is hungry.
Such is your friend's plight at midnight.
He has no food. He wakes you.
You're in a foul mood. Little wonder.
Still, you rise from your bed and
give him the bread—
not because he is your brother;
rather, because he is a bother.

...Give us this day our daily bread. [1]

And, so it is. The Door opens not because you are worthy.
It won't budge an inch even when you've fulfilled your task.
You're only received because you ask.

Seek and ye shall find; knock, and it shall be opened... [2]

Would you give a stone or scorpion to your son?
Of course not! We give only good gifts to our children.
Jesus is calling: "Here, partake of Me.
Fill up with Good and not Evil.
Holy Spirit, breathe on thee."

Blessed are those that hear God's Word and keep it. [3]

The evil generation seeks a sign, but only one is given.
Read Jonah. What do you see?
It's a whale of a tale about a city,
a man, a "great fish," [4] and forgiveness.
An unforgiving Jonah hid his light in a secret place,

(Continued)

but God made *His* own light to shine on the pagan city of Nineveh.
Jonah was in over his head when he purposely fled the wrong way
and was made to take a three-day journey in a fish's belly.
Just in time, Jonah was turned around, and the whole city repented.

...And forgive us our sins; for we also forgive every one that is indebted to us... [1]

Then, there was the Pharisee's legalistic quandary.
It's a tale without and within.
He washed the cup's rim,
then filled his insides with sin.
Not a good thing.

...And lead us not into temptation... [1]

There were the Law Keepers, too, who didn't have a clue.
They burdened their fellowman with grief beyond measure.
Now, they are condemned forever—for theft and for murder.
Generation to generation, such are the false priests of men.
Look, there's blood on each and every one of them.
They tried to steal the key hanging on the Doorpost,
and in so doing, they grieved the Holy Ghost.
Jesus said: "From the foundation of the world, they have
killed my prophets..." [5]

...but deliver us from all evil... [1]

But, *what* is the *Sign?*
Ah, yes—*that.* The one and only Sign.
At a very high cost, it made its mark,
fashioned from this Carpenter's heart.
It was not finished in gold or silver.
No, not even bronze—only wood.
It was a living tree.
Prepared and hewn. Lashed and nailed.
Trodden and torn. Rent in two.
Jesus said: "It required all of *Me* and nothing of you."
"Father, forgive them, for they know not what they do." [6]

"For thine is the kingdom and the power and the glory forever. Amen." [7]

1. Luk 11:2-4; 2. Luk 11:9-10; 3. Luk 11:28; 4. Jon 1:17;
5. Luk 11:50; 6. Luk 23:34; 7. Mat 6:13.

...And I turned to see the voice that spake with me. And being turned, I saw seven golden candlesticks; And in the midst of the seven candlesticks one like unto the Son of man...And he had in his right hand seven stars: and out of his mouth went a sharp two-edged sword: and his countenance was as the sun shineth in his strength...[He said] "Fear not; I am the first and the last: I am he that liveth, and was dead; and, behold, I am alive for evermore, Amen; and have the keys of hell and of death...The mystery of the seven stars which thou sawest in my right hand, and the seven golden candlesticks. The seven stars are the angels of the seven churches: and the seven candlesticks which thou sawest are the seven churches." (Rev 1:10, 12-20)

Interestingly, like the original seven churches in Revelation, there are seven "authentic" Christian denominations in these modern times, along with thousands of offshoots from each. All remain under the Christian "umbrella" so long as they adhere to the essential tenets of the faith.

To understand this, it is helpful to look past the differences in the various Christian denominations and focus instead on the core beliefs that are central to all of them. These beliefs are known as the *Doctrine of Christ* and have remained constant since Jesus walked the earth. Even though cultures and traditions have changed through the centuries, the *Doctrine of Christ* has not.

This *Doctrine* reflects the major points of Christ's teachings while He was here on earth, and they have been retained in the three historical "creeds" recognized, accepted, and followed by *all* true Christian denominations in the Western world. These are the *Apostles Creed*, the *Nicene Creed*, and the *Athanasian Creed*.

By adhering to the *Doctrine*, all Christian denominations come together in unity to embrace, affirm, and proclaim the "mighty wonder workings" of our Lord God and Savior, Jesus Christ. This includes Who He is, why He came to earth, the events surrounding His birth, life, death, and resurrection, and our responsibilities as His followers.

In this modern day the Lord has given us a variety of Christian denominations. The most important factor in choosing one is that whatever church you pick should follow the tenets of the faith. Remember, no church or denomination is perfect. If we try, we can find fault with all of them—even the *non*-denominational ones. If you read Revelation, you will see that Jesus found each of the original churches lacking. Even though your church may not be perfect, the Lord *is*, and He is the One Who established these seven denominations in the first place, along with all their various and sundry offshoots.

A preacher once said: "If you want to worship God, go to church. If you want to find God, read your Bible." The Lord requires us to do both. Just be sure the church you choose is God-filled and teaches and practices the unadulterated *Doctrine of Christ*.

Bible Study: 1Ch 16:22-27; Ecc 11:1-6; Isa 4:1-3, 30:25-30, 44:1-5; Jer 15:9-11; Amo 5:8; Mic 5:5, 8; Zec 4:1-14; Mat 15:34, 37, 16:10-11, 22:25-33; Mar 8:14-20; Joh 3:16; Act 6:1-7; 1Co 13:12; 1Jo 1:1-4, 2:18-27; Rev 1:1-8, 11-20, 2:1, 3:1, 4:5, 5:1-10.

Mystery of the Seven

The Bible speaks of seven lamps with God's eyes
going to and fro throughout the earth in sheer disguise,
even before the Veil was rent, even before
God had sent His Only Son into the world.

Behold, there are seven candlesticks of gold
and a bowl of purest oil above these seven lamps
bearing the cross of Christ, sealed and stamped
upon two anointed altars.

After Christ's Resurrection, the Lord sent His seven angels
to transform the seven churches spoken of in the Book of Revelation.

Where might these Seven in our modern day be?
Fast forward through the corridors of history
where they have become seven major Christian denominations,
each with thousands upon thousands of variations.

Through Christ's pure Grace, all can be traced to a common core.
Catholic/Orthodox. Episcopalian/Anglican. But, wait, there's more.
Lutheran. Presbyterian. Methodist.
Baptist/Southern Baptist/Adventists.
And last, Church of God/Pentecostals.

In all the multitude of houses bearing the Cross and Steeple,
gather two billion of God's holy people.
When it's all said and done,
all true modern Christian churches every one,
that were birthed on Earth and made in Heaven,
originated from the biblical *Seven.*

What makes them uniform?
They're all spiritually wrapped in the Virgin Born—
The Messiah. The Savior. The King.
These churches may be different in their renditions
of ritual, custom, and tradition,
yet all remain the same in their main affiliation,
which is worshiping and praising the LORD in all His names.

Though all Seven still only see "through a glass darkly,"
the Word reflects starkly in one and all
the mystery that saves us from the Fall—
the mystery that is the *Doctrine* of the Christ.

It's very simple, wouldn't you agree?
The Bible prophetically tells us what will be.
But, be wary, for we're not yet home free.
The Word also warns of the Great Apostasy.

And Jesus came and spake unto them, saying, All power is given unto me in heaven and in earth. Go ye therefore, and teach all nations, baptizing them in the name of the Father, and of the Son, and of the Holy Ghost: Teaching them to observe all things whatsoever I have commanded you: and, lo, I am with you always, even unto the end of the world. Amen. (Mat 28:18-20)

This poem was written for my brother, David (Greg) Bullard, a cancer survivor. He is only 14 months older than I am. As his little sister, I was always tagging close behind him. Now, as adults, we live 3000 miles apart, but we've still remained close over the years. When we were growing up, my father's job in the military caused us to travel quite a bit. It was a wonderful life, and we have many great memories of traveling the world together.

It was late in his life before my brother was baptized. That was several years ago. Today, in his "golden" years, he remains very active in his church, including teaching Sunday School, working on several committees, and singing in the choir. He also helps raise four of his grandchildren. The Lord has truly blessed him in so many ways.

Baptism is a public proclamation of a very personal spiritual transformation. It lets others who are saved know you, too, have accepted Christ. Traditionally, records of baptism have been kept on church roles and in family Bibles. It is evidence of those who have given their hearts and lives to the Lord. There is a comfort in having this knowledge when our loved ones pass on.

Most of all, the act of baptism proclaims your faith, belief, acceptance, and love of the One Who died for you. It is the first step in fulfilling the Great Commission for which Jesus has called all Christians—that is, proclaiming His word to "every creature" throughout the world (Mar 16:15).

If you're saved and haven't been baptized, what are you waiting for? Jesus doesn't ask much of us when we become believers, but one requirement is to come on profession of faith and be baptized. Yes, it is a Christian requirement, but it is also an honor and a privilege.

To Greg, my brother, and his wife, Brenda, with much affection and love.

And, to Jake, who was 9 years old when he was baptized
and to his sister, Kate, who is also strong in the faith.

*You are sealed by the Holy Spirit in baptism
and marked as Christ's own forever.*—Anon.

Bible Study: Mat 3:11-16, 20:22-23; Mar 1:8-9, 16:15-16; Luk 3:12-21, 7:30, 12:50; Joh 1:25-33, 3:22-26; Act 1:5, 2:38-41, 19:3-5, 22:16.

A Good Old-Fashioned Dunking

At first, I thought: "Hey, what's the big deal?
It's just a good, old-fashioned dunking."
For sure, it was a long time in coming.
But, then I realized, the Son of Righteousness
was shining in the church that morning—that Sunday.

Have thine own way, Lord. Have thine own way…

White robes of righteousness.
A baptismal font of eternal waters.
I was washed in blessings overflowing.
What can I say? Jesus took my breath away.

Thou art the potter. I am the clay…

Coming on profession of faith,
I count myself blessed.
He has saved me. He has raised me.
He has healed me through and through.
He has touched me, and I am filled.

Mold me and make me after thy will…

I remember saying: "Dear Lord,
I come foremost in obedience to You,
being baptized in the name of the Father and the Son,
and the Holy Ghost, too."
I breathed a deep sigh and in the twinkling of an eye,
I was immersed in His cleansing waters
and blanketed in His comforting verse.
What a blessing! What a thrill!

While I am waiting, yielded and still…

I've now been washed in the blood of the Lamb,
and will remain forever in the presence of the Great I AM.
Thank you, Jesus, for making me whole,
and when the roll is called up yonder,
thank you for including me there.
Hallelujah. Praise the Lord. I was baptized today
in the good, old-fashioned way.

Hold o'er my being absolute sway…
Have thine own way, Lord, have thine own way…[1]

1. Excerpts from hymn, *Have Thine Own Way, Lord* by A.A. Pollard & G.C. Stebbins, 1907.

Separation

The Reality of Hell

For God so loved the world, that he gave his only begotten Son, that whosoever believeth in him should not perish, but have everlasting life. For God sent not his Son into the world to condemn the world; but that the world through him might be saved. He that believeth on him is not condemned: but he that believeth not is condemned already, because he hath not believed in the name of the only begotten Son of God. (Joh 3:16-18)

Where Are All These People Going?

Therefore hell hath enlarged herself, and opened her mouth without measure: and their glory, and their multitude, and their pomp, and he that rejoiceth, shall descend into it. (Isa 5:14)

My dear Christian mother was concerned for close family members and friends who were not believers. She constantly kept them in her prayers. Not long after she died, I had a disturbing dream. In the stillness of the early morning, right before waking, I saw the face of an angel high above me.

"Where are all these people going?" he asked, his voice gentle, yet pensive. His question seemed to be all around me in my dream. Soundlessly, floating in thoughts, his words settled in my soul as they dropped from the air, lamenting and mournful. "I am waiting and watching," he continued, "as the unrepentant ones go this way and that, but never on the straight and narrow path."

And then, the image of the heavenly face suddenly disappeared, and a hole opened up—a big, wide, gaping hole fathoms deep in the center of the earth. Inside was a swirling, rushing fiery mass of lava and brimstone. I turned and looked over my shoulder. There, foolishly moving towards this chasm were smiling faces—laughing faces—crowded together, unwittingly moving closer and closer to the precipice. As they neared the edge, I could hear the garbled sounds of generations upon generations of voices emanating from the abyss. Suddenly, the new arrivals were caught up in the midst of that gushing whirlpool of brimstone, melding with the clamoring, babbling voices of those already there. The final result was a single, dissonant chorus, turning and churning in that hellish brine at the earth's core.

"Where are these people going?" The question hung in the air and stayed there. I looked inside the bottomless pit and saw thousands upon thousands of eyes—eyes in strange faces and some in familiar faces. These were the eyes of the unsaved dead. Unredeemed in the physical, they were now dissolving into this chaotic chasm of the spiritual where lost souls go for an eternity. They spiraled down—down into a holocaust of eternal pain and suffering where there was no respite for the weary, no balm for the tormented, and no peace for the wretched. There was only the perpetual agony of the condemned.

I awoke suddenly in a cold sweat. I remember feeling as though the responsibility of Mama's prayer vigils was being passed to me. If only the unsaved knew what awaits them after death. Yet, there are even preachers in the pulpit who avoid talking about the spiritual reality of denying Christ. Worse still, I once heard an irresponsible preacher say, "I believe there is no hell in the afterlife—that you make your own hell here on this earth." God help him and those who listen to him! Has he not read the Word? Has he not heard? Hell is as definitive and concrete and active as the boiling crucibles in a steel factory. It is the spiritual destination of the unrepentant—the damned of this world—where they will go for eternity.

Newton's *Third Law of Physics* states: "For every action, there is an equal and opposite reaction." In the physical, where there's life, there's also death. Where there's good, there's also evil. It is the same in the spiritual realm. If there is Heaven, there must also be Hell. Everyone on this earth has but two choices regarding their spiritual destination. While we are still alive, we must all respond to what is presented us regarding Christ—that is, we can either accept Him and the Grace He offers or we can reject Him. (Keep in mind, "sitting on the fence" equates to rejecting Him.) When all is said and done, there will be a very specific "eternal reaction" to your spiritual decision. After you die, you will receive either judgment or mercy. The choice is up to you.

The safest road to hell is the gradual one—the gentle slope, soft underfoot,
without sudden turnings, without milestones, without signposts.—C.S. Lewis

And there were also two other, malefactors, led with him to be put to death...And one of the malefactors which were hanged railed on him, saying, If thou be Christ, save thyself and us. But the other answering rebuked him, saying, Dost not thou fear God, seeing thou art in the same condemnation? And we indeed justly; for we receive the due reward of our deeds: but this man hath done nothing amiss.

And he said unto Jesus, 'Lord, remember me when thou comest into thy kingdom.' And Jesus said unto him, 'Verily I say unto thee, Today shalt thou be with me in paradise.' And it was about the sixth hour, and there was a darkness over all the earth until the ninth hour. And the sun was darkened, and the veil of the temple was rent in the midst. And when Jesus had cried with a loud voice, he said, 'Father, into thy hands I commend my spirit': and having said thus, he gave up the ghost. (Luk 23: 32, 39-46)

The story of these two men moves me every time I read it. Here is the living God dying on a cross for our sins, and one of the two men dying next to Him refuses to accept the Grace He offers for eternal life. Even worse, the man denigrates the Lord. This unrepentant "malefactor" is about to lose his very soul for all eternity because of the hardness of his heart. Yet, he remains in denial to the very end.

We all have known people like this—those who reject the very thing that can help them and therefore end up in the direst of circumstances. Contrast this to the other man on a cross next to Jesus. He, too, was full of sin and now at the very end of his life. Yet, when confronted with Christ, He acknowledged the Lord and repented. These two men, both thieves and felons and both about to die, choose two distinctly different paths in death. One is going to Heaven and the other to Hell.

There are two things we can learn from the remorseful man: 1) If we have a repentant heart and are willing to accept Christ, He takes us just as we are; and 2) As long as we are still alive, *it is never too late* to accept Christ.

Yes, our Lord is a God of mercy and tenderness. But, in order to reap the benefits of His grace, we must first come unto Him in repentance and ask His forgiveness. Then, the Bible says, when we forsake our wickedness and our unrighteous thoughts and turn unto Him, the Lord will have mercy and pardon us (Isa 55:7).

You won't ever find another deal better than this one! So, you should take it while you still can, for this deal has an "expiration date."

Bible Study: Pro 9:18, 15:24; Isa 5:14, 14:9, 30:21, 35:8, 40:3, 45:21; Mat 3:3, 5:22, 29-30, 7:14, 10:28, 11:10, 21:19, 23:33, 27:38; Mar 11:4, 15:27; Luk 5:12, 16:23, 23:26-46; Joh 8:21, 14:6, 19:17-18; Act 2:28, 31; Rom 3:12; 1Co 12:31; Col 2:13-15; 1Th 3:11; Heb 10:20; 2Pe 2: 1-21; Jde 1:11; Rev 1:18, 6:8, 15:3, 20:13-14.

Two Other Men on a Cross

If any man will come after me, let him deny himself,
and take up his cross, and follow me. (Mat 16:24)

There were two other men on a cross that day 2000 years ago,
one on either side of Jesus as He hung there, His soul so low,
with His body ravaged and His back all bowed.

Before their death, one looked up and acknowledged Him.
The other preferred to continue in his rejection and sin.
The one that acknowledged our LORD
went on to Paradise that very day.
The other went another way.

And so it continues to these latter days.
Death gives us the choice of just two ways.
One leads through heaven's door.
The other leads to hellfire, damnation,
and so much more.

Tell them, the LORD says, so they will know.
Lead them in the way they should go.
If they won't listen, they will have only themselves to blame,
when the doors are shut to Christ's heavenly plane.

There were two other men on a cross that day.
One went to Heaven and, sad to say,
one went the other way.

Seek ye the LORD while he may be found, call ye upon him while he is near… (Isa 55:6)

He that is unjust, let him be unjust still: and he which is filthy, let him be filthy still: and he that is righteous, let him be righteous still: and he that is holy, let him be holy still. And, behold, I come quickly; and my reward is with me, to give every man according as his work shall be. I am Alpha and Omega, the beginning and the end, the first and the last. (Rev 22:11-13)

There are so many in the younger generation who have gone over to the "dark side." The Bible calls them the "thorns and briers" (Isa 32:13). They have "gone the way of the flesh" by adorning themselves with tattoos and piercings, sporting strange hairdos, cutting themselves, drinking excessively, popping pills, puffing weed, sniffing cocaine, shooting heroin, and using sex as a form of casual entertainment.

All we can do is reach out to them and tell them about Jesus. As Christians, we are held accountable for telling others about Christ. We are to be their "wake-up call." Yet, we do not know who has a pliable heart—only the Lord knows that. Therefore, the Bible tells us we are not accountable if they will not listen. But, we can pray. Pray with them if they will and keep them in our daily prayers. Do all you can, as Jude would say, to "pull them out of the fire" (Jde 1:23). And, if you have children of your own, do your best to raise them so they will not be counted among these lost "thorns and briers."

Bible Study: Pro 23:20; Ecc 4:5, 11:10; Isa 40:6; Mat 7:7-8, 24:22, 37-38, 26:41; Mar 14:38; Luk 11:9-10, 13:25-38; 1Co 15:50; 2Co 7:1; Gal 5:1, 13, 16-26, 6:8; 1Pe 2:11, 3:21, 4:2; 2Pe 2:10, 18; 1Jo 4:2-3; Jde 1:7-8, 23; Rev 3:20, 22:1-21.

The Lost Generation

In your youthful mind, peer acceptance is popping pills,
dropping acid, puffing a grass phantasm, and
staying afloat on wild mushrooms.

Now, you're smokin'—
now, you're chillin'—
you're real cool and life is smooth.
You've drawn a line of demarcation
that shuts out the older generation.

You've left us to our more narrow space,
and gone to a place where we won't follow.
It's a place of all-consuming licentiousness,
punctuated by an excess of techno garble, dancing neon,
and deafening decibels of unintelligible sounds.

It's a place of degradation and deprivation where
no comfort, no hope, no grace can be found—
where chaos, disillusion, and confusion abound.

Before you left,
you didn't ask, so the Gift was not given.
You didn't seek, and Truth was forsaken.
You never knocked and so it goes—
the Door was locked forever.

Now, you just eat and drink and think you're merry.
And so it goes and so it goes—
until they lay you in the ground.
Welcome to the lost generation.

Kiss the Son, lest he be angry, and ye perish from the way, when his wrath is kindled but a little. Blessed are all they that put their trust in him. (Psa 12:2)

The above prophetic verse was written by King David one thousand years before Jesus Christ, the Son of God, came to earth. It is a blessing for those who would accept the Lord's magnanimous offer of redemption, as well as a warning to those who would reject it.

Eternal salvation is a gift presented to each of us by the Lord Jesus Christ. Whether or not you accept it is entirely up to you. Keep in mind, the Lord has given us all one major stipulation —we must decide *before* we die. Afterwards, it's too late. There is an old expression: "Once it is writ, it is writ." That's it. Game over. In other words, it can't be changed.

Accepting Jesus Christ as your Lord and Savior while still on this earth is the only choice you'll ever make that has eternal consequences. Once made, your choice is everlasting, non-negotiable, and permanently "cemented" with no way out. Once you die physically, the choice you made while living is what you will "live with" in the afterlife of the spiritual. Either you accept the offer Jesus Christ has made while you are in the here and now, or you lose your very soul forever on the other side. For sure, it is something to think about.

Bible Study: Gen 1:1; 28:66; Psa 1:1-6, 2:1-12; Pro 3:1-8, 30:1-9; Mat 8:26, 13:58, 14:31, 21:21; Mar 4:40, 9:24, 11:23, 16:16; Luk 14:23; Joh 1:1-5, 14, 3:16, 10:1-15, 30, 42, 14:1-7, 27-29, 20:27; Act 4:25-26; Jam 1:6; Heb 11:6, Jde 1:22; Rev 22.

To the Aging Doubter, Agnostic, and Atheist: Something to Think About

Oh, I think I understand, my man.
Methinks, you do "protest too much."
When we get older and time is running out,
it's easy to question, even to doubt:
"Did I make the right choices?"
"Do I *really* know what life is all about?"

The truth is, in the end,
when it's all said and done,
the Lord will make the final choice
for each and every one.
Before that happens to you, however,
it would be wise to ensure in your spiritual endeavor,
that, in the Father's eyes, you are in His Son's good graces.

It would be good for you to understand, my man,
that there is so much more to Infinity
than Nothingness and empty spaces,
and that the sum of Eternity's everlasting parts has been divided
into two vastly separate and distinctly different places.

The preacher sought to find out acceptable words: and that which was written was upright, even words of truth...And further, by these, my son, be admonished: of making many books there is no end; and much study is a weariness of the flesh. Let us hear the conclusion of the whole matter: Fear God, and keep his commandments: for this is the whole duty of man. For God shall bring every work into judgment, with every secret thing, whether it be good, or whether it be evil. (Ecc 12:10, 12-14)

From the study of Ecclesiastes, some modern-day theologians have come to the conclusion that its author, King Solomon, came to doubt the very God He served. So many have written about this subject that a debate continues regarding whether or not Solomon still believed in God at the end of his life. Even the famous writer, Ernest Hemingway, was enamored of Solomon's writings because he viewed them as kin to his own agnosticism and depression. He read Ecclesiastes faithfully every day to shore up his own flawed philosophy.

After careful study of King Solomon's beautiful writings, however, I could not come to the conclusion that Solomon somehow became agnostic. Yes, it is clear he had bouts of depression at times, but so did his father—King David—and David never doubted God. In addition, with so many foreign wives, Solomon was subjected to all kinds of different pagan belief systems, and he thoroughly examines some of these in certain passages. To some people, such examination could easily be mistaken for "doubting." That said, whatever doubts Solomon may or may not have had, it is evident by the last chapter of Ecclesiastes that he had resolved them.

The last three verses of Chapter 12 demonstrate beyond "a shadow of a doubt" that Solomon did not reject the Lord. In fact, it is clear God was with Him throughout His blessed and fruitful life. Even though he may have gotten "off course" a little, this man who was considered the "wisest in all the world" remained faithful to the Lord all the way to the end.

In contrast, sad to say, the "modern poet" in my poem refuses to acknowledge both God the Father as Creator of the Universe and God the Son, Jesus Christ, as his Lord and Savior. This "modern poet" is very aware of what the Bible says, and yet he still views it as a series of "fables" designed to portray a fictional god who never existed.

We know what Jesus said. What would you say to this "modern poet" if you met him?

Bible Study: Ecc 3:19; Mat 16:24-27; 22:8-14; 23:31-39; Mar 3:28-29; Joh 5:24-30; Rom 6:23; 13:1-2; 2Pe 2:1-9; Rev 22.

Stranded: Ode to the Most Modern Poet

[Jesus said] Go thy way; and as thou hast believed,
so be it done unto thee. (Mat 8:13)

The Most Modern Poet made his living
with a curmudgeon view of reality.
"Vanity, all is vanity," the Poet incessantly cried,
mindlessly echoing the lines of the Ancient Prophet.[1]
All the while, the Poet gained a lifetime of worldly recognition,
without ever truly knowing the meaning of his words.

Yet, he was haunted by another Voice from another time:
"And what shall it profit a man if he shall gain the whole world,
and lose his own soul?" [2]
Still, the Most Modern Poet remained
on his Ferris wheel of fame—
always spinning, but never really comprehending.

To be so liberally lost in thought as this renowned Poet
is quite conventional for our modern times.
But, is this the mark of genius in a mighty man of letters
or the pride and arrogance of a blind, spiritual ignorance
that precedes the Fall?

Has he never looked beyond the atmospheric covering
of this mortal realm and wondered at the width
and breadth and depth and being of the
One Who made it all?

Could he live on this planet,
shaped and fashioned long ago in the hot, fiery furnaces
of the Originator's handiwork,
without wisely weighing the worth of words
measured and meted out in the Holy Book?

Could he twirl about in this world,
thinking it is held together by only the invisible nails and
clamps and hooks of an iron-clad civilization,
never inquiring about the underlying
Mystery of it all?

(Continued)

Why would such a beautiful mind not be willing to consider
the substance and being of his unseen Maker,
but rather totally disregard and disdain the Creator
Who resides far above the boundaries of this earth's
penitentiary prism?

Could it be that such a person would go through life
in its entirety upside down and backwards,
believing in *less* rather than in *more*?
If so, is this not a type of madness in itself?

Has the Modern Poet not seen? Has he not heard?
The future is bleak for bleeding hearts.
Their fate will be to lie awash on an eternal seashore,
void of pebbles or grains of sand, looking up
at a blank, black sky at midnight—
not ever knowing where the lights have gone.

In an instant, the moon and stars will remove from their places,
exiting center stage for the glory of the One Light
that shines brighter than the noonday sun.
Still, the Most Modern Poet mimics the Ancient One
without ever understanding—
like a monkey inanely aping the actions of a man.
"Vanity," the Poet parodies over and over again,
using different sounds of syllables and altered nuances,
"All is vanity."

He does not want to hear. He does not wish to see.
All the same, he has been told the Truth.
There is no self-redemption. There is no little god within.
There never was. The only requirement put on him:
To acknowledge the Maker of it all,
and the Benefactor of Eternal Life.

Yet, he would not, and now it is too late.
The Most Modern Poet has died.
He is now stranded in a hollow space, in a separate place
where there is "weeping and gnashing of teeth." [3]
Here he will reside in this Hell of his own making for Eternity.

1. Ecc 1:2; 2. Mar 8:36; 3. Mat 25:30.

Take ye heed, watch and pray: for ye know not when the time is. For the Son of Man is as a man taking a far journey, who left his house, and gave authority to his servants, and to every man his work, and commanded the porter to watch. Watch ye therefore: for ye know not when the master of the house cometh, at even, or at midnight, or at the cockcrowing, or in the morning: Lest coming suddenly he find you sleeping. And what I say unto you I say unto all, Watch. (Mar 13:33-37)

This is a poem I wrote after the devastating *Global Financial Crisis* of 2008. It is a "What If" scenario from the point of view of "the lost." What if something even more catastrophic were to happen in America and what if the Lord were to return in the midst of it all? What would happen to those who are on the "wrong side" of God?

The idea for the poem came to me as I was with my family at a popular Italian restaurant in Seattle. Waiting for a table, it was much too noisy to have a conversation so I scanned the memorabilia on the shelves along the wall. A small white statue of a she-wolf with two male human infants caught my eye. Immediately I recognized the famous *Capitoline Wolf*, a symbol of ancient Rome. The twins on the statue, Romulus and Remus, were Rome's founders.

Legend has it these infants were cast into the Tiber River by a great uncle. There they were rescued by a she-wolf that cared for them until a herdsman took them in. Whatever their beginnings, history reflects these two brothers would eventually establish what would become at the time the largest and most powerful empire in the world.

As I sat there in the restaurant, I thought about the similarities between Rome and the U.S. Centuries after its founding, the great Roman Empire would collapse due to greed and power-brokering. Growing out of the roots of Rome, modern day America has become an even more expansive political and economic machine. Some 240+ years after our own founding, are we now on course for a similar fate?

I thought of our Lord Jesus Christ, raised up in the "boondocks" of a thriving Roman Empire in a tiny place called Palestine where He would die to save mankind. I thought of how the "little gods" of Rome would eventually be toppled and replaced by the worship of our one true God. I thought, too, of how centuries later the Lord would raise up America as a Christian country in the midst of a pagan world. Then I contemplated how far we have fallen from those Christian roots. I wondered how many of us will be ready when Jesus returns. In contrast, how many will continue worshipping the "modern gods" of gold and silver?

I was lost in thought as Italian music played softly in the background, with a buzz of pleasant conversation all around and inviting odors wafting through the air. At dinner, all these thoughts faded as I enjoyed a wonderful evening with my family. Later, at home, I sketched out my ideas in writing. After many days and numerous revisions, this poem emerged.

America survived the 2008 crisis, but we don't know when the "wolf" will be "at our door" again. What will we be doing when the End comes? We should prepare for Christ's return, just as Jesus admonished us to do, and be ready before God's wrath comes down upon this world. We don't want to be like those who have turned a "deaf ear" and thus will be left behind.

Bible Study: Sos 2:10-12; Isa 25:1-12, 40:3-10; Mat 11:10, 26:42; Mar 1:2; Luk 7:27, 11:2; Jde 1:12-25; Rev 22:5-17.

Left Behind With These Gods and Their Muse

These gods and their muse—
where will they run to?
Or will they remain with us mere mortals
in distant wood and on the plain,
in this the time of our most sorrowful refrain?

The Great Domain is silent and still.
The birds have ceased their lyrical trill.
There is no wheat for man to mill.
There are no pies on the windowsill.

The money is thrown into the streets.
The wolf no longer has the teats to suckle her young.
These feckless gods hewn in stone and shaped in metal
were passed on paper, pedal by pedal
down a walled street not paved in bars of gold
as we'd been told, but in a heaping mold
of sackcloth and ashes.

Was it simply an unworthy note of ill report?
Was it done for greed or was it done for sport?
Was it truly a sign of a civilization's decline
that was out of meter and no longer in rhyme?
Should we mere mortals have been more inclined
to believe it really was the End of Time?

Were we not listening? Did we not hear?
The words of that Fellow who said,
"Birds of a feather flock together under my wing."[1]
Who once told us to forsake and not to make
the columns, the temples, and the arches for
the gods and their goddesses.
Who warned in a most serious tone never, never to sacrifice
on their cold, dark stone.

Did we turn a deaf ear? Is that why we couldn't hear?
The voice of the turtledove in the land.[2]
The lone voice crying in the middle of desert sand.[3]
The Son calling to His Father, "Thy will be done."[4]
The Voice of the Bridegroom for His Bride declaring,
"It is time, now come."[5]

1. Mat 23:37; 2. Sos 2:12; 3. Isa 40:3; 4. Mat 6:10; 5. Rev 11:12.

Comfort and Consolation

The Peace That Passes All Understanding

As the hart panteth after the water brooks, so panteth my soul after thee, O God. My soul thirsteth for God, for the living God...Why art thou cast down, O my soul? and why art thou disquieted within me? hope thou in God: for I shall yet praise him, who is the health of my countenance, and my God. (Psa 42:1-2, 11)

* * *

The LORD is my shepherd; I shall not want. He maketh me to lie down in green pastures: he leadeth me beside the still waters. He restoreth my soul: he leadeth me in the paths of righteousness for his name's sake. Yea, though I walk through the valley of the shadow of death, I will fear no evil: for thou art with me; thy rod and thy staff they comfort me. Thou preparest a table before me in the presence of mine enemies: thou anointest my head with oil; my cup runneth over. Surely goodness and mercy shall follow me all the days of my life: and I will dwell in the house of the LORD forever. (Psa 23)

In the Face of "Never"

We do not want you to be uninformed, brothers, about the hardships we suffered in the province of Asia. We were under great pressure, far beyond our ability to endure, so that we despaired even of life. Indeed, in our hearts we felt the sentence of death. But this happened that we might not rely on ourselves but on God, who raises the dead. (2Co 1:8-9)

My oldest son, Charles, e-mailed me a passage from Os Hillman's online *TGIF Daily Devotional* that included the above Bible verse. In the opening paragraph, Hillman wrote:

Have you ever gone through a very difficult time in your life? These times make us value life. They make us appreciate the simple things that we took for granted before the crisis. When we are restored from such a trial, it is as though we have been given a new beginning. We can place a greater value on what we had before and use it for His purposes. Perhaps for the first time we can identify with others who find themselves in a similar trial...

There was more, but it was the Bible verse from Corinthians as well as Hillman's question that struck me. I had also been thinking about what another preacher, Charles Stanley, had said in one of his sermons. He said we are commanded to do God's will even when it seems unreasonable to us. In other words, it's not necessary that we always *understand* God's word or directive. Instead, it's more important that we exercise *faith* to remain in God's will—even when we would rather do something different or it would be more expedient to do something else.

This verse from Corinthians is a good one to put to memory. It's the answer for all those "legalists" and "prosperity preachers" who say: "If you're having problems in your life, you must be doing something wrong. You must not be in God's will."

Somehow, I don't think those people ever read Job. For sure, they most likely haven't read the above verse by Paul, for he tells us just the opposite. Sometimes God puts us through trials in life so we can learn not to rely on ourselves, but instead to put all our faith in the Lord. Sometimes, those trials can be so great they may cause us to "despair of life" itself. Peter says when you suffer for something you did, that's not good, but suffering for God *is* a good thing (1Pe 3:11-17). And, in Hebrews, we learn that God chastises those He loves (Heb 12:6). The good news is the Lord does not discipline us simply to be mean. Like a loving father, He does it so we can grow closer to Him and learn His ways.

Even when we are faithful in all things, the "Christian walk" is not an easy one. For sure, the Lord will test us and "mold" us, sometimes even to the breaking point. But, He doesn't do this to harm us. Sometimes it's to make us stronger, and sometimes we might never know why. Still, there is one thing we *can* know. Whatever befalls us in our lifetime, the Lord will always use it for His greater purpose. As Paul tells us, our "bad" circumstances will "work together for good" in ways we can't even begin to comprehend. We can therefore be assured the Lord will *always* be there to see us through our trials and tribulations.

Quite often, however, there are people who will look at others in trouble or those who have a need and think: "Why should I listen to them? They have no blessings in their lives—or at least they appear to have none. They haven't been successful in anything. And, look at what they're going through now..."

You may know people who would think such things. From my own experience, however, I've found that those who continue in the faith even when they are in desperate straits are the ones who may be doing things right. In other words, just because someone is prosperous and successful does not necessarily mean that person is "walking the walk." If one can still "keep the faith"—even in the most difficult of circumstances—they have far more than a "surface" belief. It is these people I listen to with attentive ears and an open heart.

You might be thinking: "What if they never achieve success? Isn't that a sign something is lacking in their character or belief system?" But, I would say it's in the "face of never" when real faith emerges. It's when a person says way down deep inside that "no matter what my circumstances are, and even if those circumstances never change, I will hold fast to my faith in Jesus."

Did Job lose faith in God when he lost his children, land, wealth, health, and the respect of his wife and friends? *No.* He continued to have faith, even when his wife told him to "lie down and die." Did Moses lose faith during Israel's 40-year trek in the wilderness? Many of his followers did, but Moses did not. He remained faithful to the Lord—even when his own brother and sister questioned his God-given authority as Israel's rightful leader.

David had to live in caves to hide from King Saul who wanted to kill him. Did he lose faith in God? *No.* Even when he had the chance to kill Saul, David did not do so because the Lord had forbidden it. Jeremiah's own people threw him down the well to die. Did he lose faith in God? *No.* He made his way up and out of that well and continued on, preaching God's truth no matter what opposition he received—even from the king and his so-called fellow priests of God.

We can't forget Joseph. He suffered trials beyond comprehension, starting as a teenager when he was thrown into a pit by his own brothers and left to die. But, his suffering didn't end there. Found by a passing caravan of strangers, he was taken to Egypt to be sold as a slave. Because he remained faithful to the tenets of God's law, he was thrown into an Egyptian prison and served many years for a crime which he did not commit. After all was said and done, Joseph suffered 17 years through the prime of his youth before being released from prison. Yet, even though he was a foreigner, he would eventually be elevated to the second highest office in the land of Egypt because of his faith.

Centuries later, the Apostle Paul was a prime example of remaining faithful to God in the midst of great suffering. He experienced every hardship imaginable—from shipwrecks, beatings, and imprisonment to being challenged by his fellow Christians, including the other Apostles. Yet, never giving up, he continued taking the Gospel to the Gentiles just as the Lord had directed him.

The Apostle John was another who suffered extreme hardships before and during his imprisonment on the Isle of Patmos. All the while, he continued diligently and faithfully to complete God's directive. At roughly 90 years of age and while living in a cave as a prisoner on Patmos, his final and greatest act was to write down the Book of Revelation as it was given him directly from the Lord. This would become the last and most comprehensive book of prophecy in the Holy Bible.

There are so many other examples of how God's chosen remained faithful even in the worst of times and unto death. In the Old Testament, all the prophets suffered at the hands of God's enemies in various and sundry ways. Likewise, as recorded in the New Testament, the Twelve Apostles suffered greatly as well, with all but John being martyred. Yet, regardless of their circumstances, they remained faithful in taking God's message to the world. Not one gave up in the face of difficult circumstances—including trials, torture, imprisonment, hardship, and persecution. And, neither should we. As Paul stated: "Whether I abase or whether I abound, therewith I will be content" (Php 4:11-14).

"Content in what?" you might ask. You can be content in knowing your present "bad" circumstances do not reflect who you are, Whom you serve, or what your fate might be. You can be certain you are not being ignored by God, abandoned, or set aside. The Lord will remain with you through *all* circumstances—even unto death. If the whole world abandons you, the Lord will not, for He states emphatically in both the Old and New Testaments: "I will never leave you nor forsake you" (Deu 4:31; Heb 13:5).

In the direst of circumstances, Paul said: "I can do all things through Christ which strengthens me" (Php 4:13). You notice he didn't say "some things" or "many things" or "most things." He said *all things*. Why? As Christians, our source of strength does not come from ourselves. It comes wholly from Christ.

What about those people who witness a person going through trials? Paul says: "Notwithstanding ye have well done, that ye did communicate with my affliction" (Php 4:14). In other words, don't be like Job's friends and blame the person for his own misfortune. Don't give him even *more* heartache than he already has. Would you be like Job's wife and tell such a person they might as well "lie down and die?"

Instead, lift up their spirits. If you see others going through trials and difficult circumstances, give them empathy and concern. Offer assistance whenever you can. This is more than simply "doing good." It's a way to demonstrate our love—love for our fellow man, as well as love and appreciation for our Lord. This is the way we honor God.

Psalm 139 tells us that if we were to go down to the "depths of the sea," there we would find the Lord. If we could reach the "highest star in the heavens," there we would find God. Fortunately, we don't have to do any of that. We need not go on a pilgrimage nor do we have to do great works in order to earn His love and attention.

The Good News is, as Christians, the Lord abides right here in our hearts—in the very depths of our being through the indwelling of the Holy Spirit. He is not a distant, unfeeling God Who leaves us to our own devices. No. He remains "up close and personal"—a friend "of the most unique kind" and a helper in our time of trouble. Best of all, He has promised to be with us always—even when we go through the "valley of the shadow of death" at the end of our days. As a Christian, you can bet your life on this—both here on earth and on into eternity!

To Bernie G.,
Thanks for giving me sound counsel and biblical
wisdom in a dark time in my life. It is true.
God is always there to see us through.

I know now, Lord, why you utter no answer.
You are yourself the answer.
Before your face questions die away.
What other answer would suffice?
—C.S. Lewis

Behold, I will send my messenger, and he shall prepare the way before me: and the Lord, whom ye seek, shall suddenly come to his temple, even the messenger of the covenant... (Mal 3:1)

John the Baptist was the last of the prophets under the Old Covenant. He was prophesied in Isaiah 40:3-5 (about 740 B.C.) and in Malachi 3:1 (about 400 B.C.) as the "one voice crying in the wilderness" who would "prepare the way" for the coming Messiah. He was verified as this lone "voice" in all four Gospels, including by Jesus (Matthew 11 and Luke 7). For certain, John was prophesied as the one to herald Christ's arrival.

And, yet, there has been an ongoing discussion among many modern theologians as to whether John, while in prison and awaiting execution, had begun to doubt if Jesus really was the Messiah. If we look at the scriptural evidence, however, we can easily see that this simply was not the case.

From Scripture, we learn John received the Holy Spirit while still in Elizabeth's womb (Luk 1:15) and literally jumped when she greeted the also pregnant Virgin Mary (Luk 1:41-44). John, a Nazarite, dedicated his life to declaring Jesus as the Messiah, and Jesus designated John to baptize Him.

In John, we see a close kinsman, a true friend, and a faithful prophet heralding Jesus as "God in the flesh." He told his disciples: "...'I am not the Christ,' but, 'I have been sent before Him'...the friend of the bridegroom, who...rejoices greatly because of the bridegroom's voice...The Father loves the Son, and has given all things into His hand. He who believes in the Son has everlasting life; and he who does not believe the Son shall not see life..." (Joh 3:28-29, 35-36). In fact, John told his disciples long before he was imprisoned: "He must increase, but I *must* decrease" (Joh 3:30). This all strongly indicates that John would have had *more* faith—not less—in his time of testing.

So the question presented by John to Jesus must have served another purpose. What could it have been? In Isaiah 40, there's a hint. The prophet cries: "What am I suppose to cry—what am I suppose to prophesy?" (v.6). God gives him his answer. It is that God's glory will be "revealed before all men." Thus, John was sending his disciples to Jesus, proclaiming what was prophesied long ago: "Behold your God" (See vs. 8-9, 11-12, 26, & 28). John was sending his two trusted disciples to be eyewitnesses to the reality of Jesus as the Christ. He was saying: "Go to the source. Then you will know."

If anything, it was John's disciples that were confused and doubting—*not* John. John knew it was time, and he was lovingly sending them to follow Jesus and to lead his other disciples to Him as well.

After Jesus had spoken to the two men, He turned to the crowd and began what would be one of the most beautiful eulogies ever given. He condemned those responsible for John's impending demise while offering hope for all who would believe and follow Him. He knew what his faithful kinsman and friend must endure, as well as what He himself would suffer in the near future. The answer for John's two disciples was in the haunting question repeated over and again in Christ's eulogy for His beloved friend: "What went you out to see?

Bible Study: Gen 3:16; Isa 40:1-31; Mal 3:1-18; Mat 3:3, 11:1-30, 21:21-22; Mar 1:2-3, 8:28; Luk 3:4-6, 7:1-36, 9:62; Joh 1:23, 3:25-36.

A Eulogy of Hope
(Based on Matthew 11)

"Jesus," the two disciples of John asked,
while the Baptist awaited the Silver Platter:
"Are you the One or should we look for another?"

Jesus answered: "Go and show John what you hear and see.
Blessed is he who shall not be offended in Me.
The blind see. The lame walk. Lepers are cleansed.
The deaf hear. The dead are raised.
The poor receive the Good News."

Then, Jesus turned and spoke to the multitudes,
which included His enemies, the Pharisees.
"What went you out in the wilderness to see?
A reed blowing limply in the wind?
Instead, you found John to be a wild, yet strong and steadfast man.

What went you out to see?
A king clothed in soft raiment?
Instead, you found a man dressed in camel's hair,
young, bold, robust, and fair,
walking through dust and sand
in a rugged, untamed, desert land.

What went you out to see?
A prophet? Behold, John was so much more.
He was the messenger sent before Me.
Regarding this I will only say:
'Like Elijah, he has prepared the way.' [1]

There has not been one born of women
greater than John the Baptist, but hear this:
He that is least in Heaven's Kingdom
will be greater than John.

(Continued)

For now, on this earth,
the Kingdom of Heaven suffers violence,
and the violent have their way.
But, I say, there will come a time when this is not so.
It is called the Judgment Day. [2]

What went you out to see?
To those that have ears to hear, let them hear and receive:
Until now, all the prophets from Abraham to Elijah to John
have prophesied about the Messiah, the Righteous One,
and now He has come.

To those vipers who will not listen:
You wanted John to entertain you?
To play music so you could dance? Or, by perchance,
make you fall into a frenzied religious trance?
Or, did you need proof to believe?
Show you the evidence and *then* you would see?

And just what might that be?
You sit in the marketplace all day,
listening to hearsay and expecting to be spoon-fed the Truth.
You were told. He said that I was prophesied from old.[3]
You have been witnesses first-hand and still you do not understand.

John didn't eat or drink anything that wasn't kosher,
and you were sure he had a devil.
Yet I come eating and drinking freely, and you say
I am a glutton and a drunkard and a friend of sinners.
Haven't you heard? Faith comes by hearing,
and hearing by God's Word.[4]
Holy Spirit, breathe on My *true* children.

Woe unto you and your cities that will not receive.
You hear and see and still do not believe the works I've done in you.
Yet, if those ancient, barbarous pagans
of Tyre, Sidon, and Sodom had seen what you have seen,
they would have recognized their King.
I say unto you it will be more tolerable for those wretched souls of old
than for you at Judgment Day."

Then, Jesus turned and prayed:
"Thank you, Father, Lord of Heaven and earth,
for hiding these things from the so-called prudent and wise,
and for revealing them unto innocent babes, for this is good in Your eyes.

Father, through your might, you have given Me all I need.
Indeed, no man can know the Son, but by the Father Who sent Me.
Moreover, no man can know the Father unless he has known the Son,
and acknowledges the prophesied Righteous One.

So, what went you out to see?
Turn now and look to the Tree of Calvary.
Come, all you who are weary, with heavy burdens to carry,
for I am meek and humble and will give you rest.
Come, like John, do what is best in God's sight.
My yoke is easy and my burden light.
Read My Word as you have heard.
Come, join Me and pursue the true teachings of God."

1. Mat 17:12; 2. 2Pe 2:9; 3. Isa 40:3-31; 4. Rom 10:17.

They that go down to the sea in ships, that do business in great waters; These see the works of the Lord, and his wonders in the deep. For he commandeth, and raiseth the stormy wind, which lifteth up the waves thereof. They mount up to the heaven, they go down again to the depths: their soul is melted because of trouble. They reel to and fro, and stagger like a drunken man, and are at their wit's end. Then they cry unto the Lord in their trouble, and he bringeth them out of their distresses. He maketh the storm a calm, so that the waves thereof are still. Then are they glad because they be quiet; so he bringeth them unto their desired haven. Oh that men would praise the Lord for his goodness, and for his wonderful works to the children of men! (Psa 107:23-31)

The year 2015 marked the 10th anniversary of Hurricane Katrina. Watching all the old videos on television brought back memories of its crushing devastation. It was a terrible ordeal for those living all along the coastline of Mississippi and Louisiana. In Louisiana it was much worse, for amid the natural disaster, New Orleans' governmental infrastructure totally failed, bringing chaos, pandemonium, crime, and anarchy in its wake. Yet, in the face of it all, we could see God's helping hand working through His holy people.

The Coast Guard did a miraculous job in rescuing thousands. Doctors, nurses, and other medical personnel worked tirelessly to help the sick and disabled. Private citizens put their lives in jeopardy to save others, even in rescuing animals. Financial donations poured in from all over the world. The neighboring state of Texas opened up its doors to thousands upon thousands of the hurricane's displaced victims, sending them to locations where preparations had been made ahead of time for their own citizens in case of emergency disasters. There, the displaced masses found safe, comfortable haven, receiving much needed rest, nourishment, and refuge from the storm's aftermath. Yes, there was suffering and turmoil, but in the midst of it all, we could also see God's tender mercies.

It is in such times that we call out for God to help us. Yet, some forget they continually deny God's existence in the more peaceful days of their lives. Some forget they usually opt to tout the worship of the lesser gods of this world over the Almighty. Still others, those with an outward semblance of belief, forget they generally ignore the Lord in their daily living, very seldom acknowledging the blessings He continually bestows on them.

No matter, in terrifying times like Hurricane Katrina, these same people call upon the Lord, asking Him to save them from their perils. And, when He does—when the danger passes and life returns to normal—they once again abandon the God that saved them, quickly forgetting any promises they had made to Him in their moment of great calamity. Worse still, many blame Him for their ordeal. It's an old, old story that has been repeated since the beginning of mankind. The reason does not lie in their forgetfulness or in their mindset, but in the condition of their hearts. As Christians, let's do as the Psalm says and not go the way of the world. Let us acknowledge the Lord in all we do and continue to praise Him for His goodness and for all His wonderful works in both good times and bad.

Bible Study: Deu 4:30; Jdg 10:13-16; Job 21:18-21; Psa 55:8, 83:15, 107:22-31, 148:3-14; Isa 4:6, 25:4, 8-9, 29:6-7; Nah 1:3; Mar 4:37-41; Luk 8:23; Joh 16:33; Act 14:22; Rom 5:1-4, 8:35-39, 12:9-21; 2Co 1:3-7; 1Th 3:2-5; 2Th 1:4.

Where Have You Been?

Thou [God] rulest the raging of the sea: when the waves
thereof arise, thou stillest them. (Psa 89:9)

I met a white woman on the Mississippi Coast last Saturday.
She wasn't a ghost, but one of the living.
She had lost her way
and now had come face to face with Katrina.
She had seen Camille, too—long years ago
when she made her grand debut.
Both the woman and her house
had withstood the storm's force back then—
but, not this time.

All the poor woman could do was wail when the gale sailed through,
crying, "God, save me, *please*!"
When she fell to her knees,
her prayers were answered.
Katrina blew her house down all around her,
but *she* was still alive.

In New Orleans, I saw a sea of anguished faces
in an ocean of ravaged places.
I saw a man lying dead
where he had made his final bed
on the side of a road.
"Oh, Lord, give us this day our daily bread,"
another man had cried before he died
in the middle of Hell on the I-10 overpass.

I heard people knocking on rooftops
inside flooded houses with no way out.
"Oh God! Oh Lord!" They entreated,
and unceasingly repeated:
"Oh Christ! Where are *You*?"

I let out a long sigh,
for the Angel of Death was nigh.
There went ten more dead bodies floating by.
Again and again, the living would ask "Why?"
But again and again, there would be no answer—
not then.

(Continued)

I saw one lone man in Pass Christian
standing with a bent-up wash pan.
It was the only thing he could find
in the rubble he once called home.
"Oh, Lord, give us this day..."
he persistently prayed.

In the midst of all the dying,
I saw Coast Guard helicopters flying.
They were coming in low
in a miraculous show—
like giant locusts summoned from Heaven.

Back on the Coast as we peered down from the sky,
we could see wreckage and splintered wood piled high,
looking more like mounds of sawdust and scattered toothpicks.
"Why? Why?" the survivors continued their cry,
"Why did all these people have to die?"

If you listen to the songster,
The only answer is "blowin' in the wind,"
but, that's no more than empty writing with a pen.
For now, make your home a better place.
Teach your children about true Grace—
the Grace the woman found that day.
You remember? The sweet lady I met
on the Mississippi Coast—
the day she came face to face
with Me and the Father and the Holy Ghost.

I had been out there walking on the water,
in the wind, in the flood, in the rain—
patiently waiting for them.
They just didn't know.
I was there in the raging storm.
I was there when it was time to mourn.
I was there to care for every child.
I had been there all the while.

Still, there were not many that would hear me,
nor many who could see me.
But, the few who called My Name,
I answered them.
Yes, I could have passed them by,
and, with a sigh, been on My way.

But, I didn't. I stopped that day,
for the lady and the lone man
and for all the children.

I was there for all of them—
for the hopeless, for the weary,
for the disheveled, for the despairing.

I was there for the living, for the dead, and for the dying.
Didn't you know? I have always been here.
Where have *you* been?

For if ye forgive men their trespasses, your heavenly Father will also forgive you: But if ye forgive not men their trespasses, neither will your Father forgive your trespasses. (Mat 6:12, 14-15)

Unforgiveness is something we all wrestle with at one time or another. People can do things so unjustified, so cruel, or horrendous that it just seems there is no way you could ever forgive them. Worse still, after a while, the grudge you are holding begins to feel *comfortable*— much like a pair of old shoes. It "wears" so well you don't want to give it up. But, the Lord says for your own well-being, you must—and the sooner the better. Just as you would throw out a favorite pair of old shoes with holes in them that are ruining your arches and causing pain with every step, you must get rid of unforgiveness. Granted, this is not always easy. But, you *can* do it—with the Lord's guidance. When Jesus told the Apostles they had to learn forgiveness, they knew how difficult this would be, for their response was: "Lord, increase our faith" (Luk 17:5).

Unforgiveness causes pain and suffering mainly to just one person—the one who refuses to forgive. The "voice" in my poem is such a person. Sadly, the longer you hold on to unforgiveness, the more damage it does. A veil of despair will descend upon your spirit, and your happiness will gradually erode, replaced with a seething sense of resentment, anger, and bitterness. This will eventually rob you of all joy and well-being.

No matter how wronged you have been, your unforgiveness will not accomplish anything that is good. For sure, it will not change anyone else. It will not prevent someone from doing what they are doing or alter their thinking. They will probably go about their business as usual without caring about what they have done, even after saying they're sorry. If the issue is relational, you have to determine if you want to continue the relationship. If the issue is a crime, the law will handle it. But, regardless, the Lord says, "Vengeance is mine" (Rom 12:19). In the end, the Lord will deal with that person. My mother used to tell me: "Don't worry. That person will get their just desserts. God will see to that. Just let it go." It's important to live in God's will and be concerned with being in the right relationship with Him. With that will come joy, peace, understanding, and forgiveness.

There are many passages in the Bible dealing with anger and unforgiveness. The Bible Study below touches on quite a few of these related passages. Paul says: "Don't let the sun go down on your wrath" (Eph 4:26). That is because if you let anger simmer, it will eventually take root deep within your soul. Worse still, if we don't forgive others, Jesus tells us, our Father in heaven will not forgive us. As Christians, we are not even supposed to take communion unless we have forgiven those who have wronged us. Thus, we want to be quick to forgive so as to remain in a right relationship with the Lord.

If you have unforgiveness in your heart toward anyone, let it go this very day. If it takes hold of your spirit—as it did for the person in this poem—it will adversely affect your life in the "here and now" and possibly forever. It's just not worth it. Remember what Jesus said on the Cross: "Father, forgive them, for they know not what they do" (Luk 23:34). Jesus is "faithful and just" to forgive us our sins. Shouldn't we do the same for others?

Bible Study: Gen 50:17; Exo 10:17, 32:32; Psa 37:8; Pro 15:18, 16:32; Mat 5:25, 6:12-15, 9:6, 18:15, 21-35, 27:61; Mar 3:29, 11:25-26; Luk 6:37, 11:4, 17:1-5, 23:44; Act 8:21-23; Rom 12: 2, 19; 2Co 2:7, 10; Gal 6:1-18; Php 4:6-7, 13; Col 3:13-14; Eph 4:26-27, 31-32.

Unforgiveness

There you go again!
You've hurt my feelings—
laid them open and exposed.
Pricked. Pained. Bleeding.

The words remain,
floating in wounds
so raw and seething
that I want to cry.
But, I won't.

Instead, I pull them in and lick them,
like a cat washing herself.
I need no anesthetic for this pain.
No Balm or Ointment for healing.

Over time, the wounds will mend.
They always do.
But, the scars will be there forever,
along with the pain—especially the pain.

It's deep inside now,
in the dark recesses of my soul,
churning and turning into bitterness and anguish,
for I have refused to let it go.

Hast thou not known? hast thou not heard, that the everlasting God, the Lord, the Creator of the ends of the earth, fainteth not, neither is weary? there is no searching of his understanding. He giveth power to the faint; and to them that have no might he increaseth strength. Even the youths shall faint and be weary, and the young men shall utterly fall: But they that wait upon the Lord shall renew their strength; they shall mount up with wings as eagles... (Isa 40:28-31)

In an online *TGIF Daily Devotional*, Os Hillman noted the desert is "often a still place" and yet it is also where "the devil will speak loudest." These words resonated deep in my heart and became the inspiration for this poem.

The Lord says that He will "never leave you nor forsake you" (Heb 13:5). Yet, time and again, when we find ourselves in a "desert of our lives," we move further away from God instead of closer. As our despair deepens, we may turn into ourselves, shutting out not only our family and friends, but also the Lord. It's then the Devil can really work on us. But, we don't have to let that happen. We don't have to get to that point. All we need to do is call on the One Who can take care of any circumstance, trial, or tragedy in our lives.

If you call on the name of Jesus, you can be assured He will be there. Trust on Him, believe in Him, and accept Him at His Word. He will see you through any adversity that ol' Devil can throw at you. But, don't believe me. Ask Jesus. Go to Him in prayer and read His Word, the Holy Bible. If you keep the faith, the Lord will make His presence known.

With love from Aunt Debbie to my great nephew, Josh,
and all the family, Jim, Trina, Jobie, and Kristi,
and grandparents, Susie and Swede, Ron and Charlene.

"We believe in miracles."

God, who foresaw your tribulation,
has specially armed you to go through it,
not without pain but without stain.
—C.S. Lewis

"For I know the plans I have for you," declares the Lord, "plans to prosper
you and not to harm you, plans to give you hope and a future." (Jer 29:11)

Bible Study: Psa 4:2, 8:3, 18:1-3, 23:4, 25:4-6, 50:15, 55:16, 69:15-17, 71:19-24, 77:9-15, 91:4-7, 116:13, 119:46-50, 75-77, 81-83, 147:4; Pro 2:7; Isa 49:16; Jer 31:35; Amo 5:6, 8; Mat 4: 1-11; Luk 11:9; Rom 15:14; Rev 1:16, 22:13-14, 16-17.

The Devil Shouts Loudest in the Desert

We've all gone through metaphorical deserts in our lives.
Loss of loved ones. Sickness. Disease. Financial crises.
Loneliness. Despair. The list goes on.

It's in those despondent times,
the Devil will shout the loudest.
At first he may simply whisper in your ear.
But, if he doesn't get your attention,
he will begin to yell.

 "Hey, you! Where's your God?
Where is that one named Jesus?
Didn't He say He would 'never leave you nor forsake you'?[1]
So, tell me—where is He now?"

It's in those most dire moments,
we need to open our Bible.
We need to delve deep into the Word of God.
When we look for Jesus, we will find Him.
When we call out His name, He will be there.

How do we know?
It's written in His Word. It's set in the stars.
It's emblazoned in the palms of His hands.
It's illustrated on the Cross at Calvary.[2]

Yes, there will be doubt
when we're lost in the wilderness of our woes.
Yet, in the midst of our trials and troubles,
Christ will always make His presence known.
The key is in seeking Him with all our hearts.

The Bible tells us to call on Him, and He'll be there.
Jesus Himself said: "Ask, and it shall be given you.
Seek and ye shall find.
Knock and the door will be opened unto you."[3]

(Continued)

Jesus is "the Rock."
He is "our fortress, our deliverer,
and our salvation."[4]
He is "the tried stone, the precious cornerstone,
the sure foundation."[5]
With Him, we can do anything.
Without Him, we are nothing.

Even when our faith fails,
the Lord will lift us up.
We can depend on Him.
We can count on Him.
There is nothing, no temptation,
no trial in our lives
when He won't be there with us.

Through the Holy Spirit,
the Lord will pour down on us
His comfort, His peace, His tender mercies,
and His loving kindness,
giving us the ability and strength to carry on,
even in the midst of our most grievous troubles.

So, when you find yourself lost out there
in a desert of inconsolable despair,
and the Devil starts to shout his ominous words
of trepidation, fear, and doubt,
do what Christ did in His wilderness trials.
Stand on the solid, holy ground of Scripture.

Know the Word. Recite the Word.
All the while, call on the name of Jesus.
Declare your faith, hope, and trust in Him alone.
Against such odds,
you'll make that old serpent speechless.
Then, watch him turn and slither away.

1. Heb 3:5; 2. Luk 23:33; 3. Mat 7:7; 4. Psa 18:2; 5. Isa 28:16.

Regeneration

All Things Are Made New in Christ Jesus

Therefore if any man be in Christ, he is a new creature: old things are passed away; behold, all things are become new...Now then we are ambassadors for Christ...For he hath made him to be sin for us, who knew no sin; that we might be made the righteousness of God in him. (2Co 5:17, 20-21)

A Broken Vessel

And the vessel that he made of clay was marred in the hand of the potter: so he made it again another vessel, as seemed good to the potter to make it. (Jer 18:4)

A few years back, I was in the middle of a "Woe is me" syndrome and had been for quite some time. During this trying period of my own making, I hadn't been studying the Word as much as I should, and I hadn't been writing faithfully as had been my habit for many years. Truthfully, I had been quite engrossed and caught up in my own problems—wondering "why" I had to endure so much physical pain all the time and "why" I had so many health issues. The list went on and on. On top of that, I was concerned about my old age and what I was going to do with the rest of my life of 60+ years after retiring my business due to health reasons.

It seems the Lord had put me in the middle of a big lesson, and I didn't know what I was supposed to be learning. He had brought me so very far in those last few years, so I knew he wasn't going to abandon me. I had gone through a period of failing health several years before, with a great deal of pain and physical debilitation, as well as financial and emotional problems that go along with chronic illness. Then, just as I was recovering, my mother died. Not too long after, we moved across country.

Finally, after a couple of years, we were settled in our new community and things were looking up. Even though I still had physical issues, including chronic pain from fibromyalgia, my overall health had improved considerably. Our finances were good. There were no major crises in our lives. But, in the midst of all the good things, I suddenly felt overtaken with a complete sense of helplessness and futility. I knew it was an emotional thing and hoped it would pass. I kept telling myself that daily. But, still, I couldn't shake it.

Then, on one particular morning, after I had been kneeling for quite some time before the Lord, a flood of peace washed over me—the peace talked about in the Bible—the kind that "passes all understanding" (Php 4:7). While in prayer, the Lord even gave me a great idea to help jolt me out of my writer's block. From that moment, He began to show me that even though He might not take away my physical debilitation and pain completely, He would help me to live successfully (in the spiritual sense) despite my ailments. Perhaps my physical limitations were a "thorn in my side" similar to what Paul talked about, one that would be a constant reminder of how much I need and depend upon the Lord and on Him alone.

Feeling better, I picked up a book of poems. There, on the page I opened up was a quote by Henry Wadsworth Longfellow:

> Let us be up and doing
> With a heart for any fate,
> Still achieving, still pursuing,
> Learn to labor and to wait.[1]

This classic poem really made me think. Lighting up that page of poetry, I saw a message for my situation there. "Learn to labor and to wait." We need to wait on the Lord for guidance through prayer and supplication while at the same time engaging life to its fullest and not being bogged down through inaction and incessant, needless worry like I had been in those past few months. We need not be concerned about our fate if we are in God's will and fulfilling His purposes. And, we won't have time to worry and fret if we are "up and doing."

Last, we should put our whole heart into achieving and pursuing these goals until the very end of our lives. In this lifetime, we may never see the results of what God has purposed for us. But, one day in Heaven we will.

Mr. Longfellow had given me a bolt of inspiration I needed right when I needed it. It was a "Holy Spirit" moment. It was then I could feel my depression being lifted, and my physical pain lessened. It didn't happen overnight, but things gradually got better and better. Even my pain was not as bad as it had been.

I still have my moments when the clouds of darkness settle in, especially when my physical pain seems overwhelming. But now, I can look back to that particular moment in time and "see" how the Lord led me through it all. This always gives me renewed hope and the ability to overcome both the depression and the pain. Best of all, I know where to go. Just as the hymn says: "Where can I go but to the Lord!"

It's the tender mercies and grace bestowed upon us by the Lord Jesus that heals us spiritually and puts us back together again better than ever! In order to be truly healed emotionally, our inner wounds have to be exposed to the Light of the Lord through continual prayer and supplication. And, it's in the repairing of our broken-*ness* that He teaches us to have mercy and empathy for others. In so doing, we learn to release the negativity that defines us in those dark hours and just let it go. As often is the case, however, we can easily fall back into the negativity all over again if we don't continue in the Word. The good news is, when we go before the Lord asking sincerely for release and repentance, the festering spiritual "germs and bacteria" that fill our souls in the form of despair, depression, hopelessness, misery, heartache, bitterness, resentment, anger, and most of all—unforgiveness—are cleansed from deep down inside our hearts.

Then and only then can we be truly healed spiritually for, in effect, it is the Lord's forgiveness that drills like a laser beam deep into a repentant, pliable heart. It is only through this process the miracle of true change can occur. Like a surgeon repairing the heart, Christ works on our spirit to bind us together again and make us whole. He then carefully places us where we best fit into His heavenly mosaic patchwork design. As the Bible tells us, the only way we can truly know Christ is to lose ourselves in Him.

After we've been put back together again, we start living not of ourselves, but for Christ—no matter what our circumstances. We stop thinking in terms of what satisfies us. Instead, we begin thinking in terms of what is pleasing to Christ. As the Lord searches our hearts, our spirits may need tweaking now and again, sometimes in big ways and sometimes in small ways. After all, "Christianity is not a destination, but a life-long journey." Eventually, when we get to Heaven, we will be complete. It is there we will become part of God's beautiful mosaic of perfect goodness and love.

From Aunt Debbie with love,
To Kim & Rick, Rachel, Michaela & Skye
Bob, Jack, and Maddie
Craig, Wanda, Debbie, and family
Karla and family

Our hearts in big and small ways
can keep God's love that keeps us strong.
—*Friends Are Friends Forever*, Song by Michael W. Smith

1. Henry Wadsworth Longfellow, *A Psalm of Life*

Let us hear the conclusion of the whole matter: Fear God, and keep his commandments: for this is the whole duty of man. For God shall bring every work into judgment, with every secret thing, whether it be good, or whether it be evil. (Ecc 12:13-14)

Warning! This poem is not for the faint of heart.

This narrative poem is one that came to me in the middle of the night, and I had to get up and immediately write it down. It's about some of the many sins we usually don't want to talk about. You might say it's a reality check. The surprise is at the end as you gradually realize who the narrator is. Or, you may even guess it from the beginning. Most importantly, this poem, even though it may not sound like it at first, is not a poem of condemnation. Rather, it is a poem of grace, love, mercy, and forgiveness.

If you read all the Bible Study verses that accompany it, you will literally take a quick jog through the Bible regarding "doctrine, reproof, and instruction" (2Ti 3:16). Even though God's Word is absolute and resolute, it is also filled to overflowing with grace, love, mercy, and tenderness. Following Christ is a choice. You can choose either to accept His grace that is offered or reject it. Keep in mind, rejecting Christ's offer has its own set of consequences for the individual, here in this life and in the life to come. Sadly, we move further away from the Lord when we don't take His Word to heart and decide to live according to this world rather than obeying God's laws and commandments.

What we often forget is that God's Word was not set forth to prevent us from enjoying life and finding happiness. It's just the opposite. God gave us His own personal instructional guide called the Holy Bible so we can live a joyful, productive, purpose-filled life in prosperity and wellness with the least amount of adversity. The problem is we always manage to let "self" get in the way.

Bible Study: Gen 2-4, 22:1-14, 24:40, 26:34-35; Jos 3:5; 2Sa 11:1-27, 12:1-7; Psa 1:1-6; 23:1-6; 119:99-106; Pro 1-10, 13:10, 17:10-14, 22:10, 24:13; Isa 7:14-15, 28:9-11; Jer 29:11-39; Mat 7:7-8, 28:20; Joh 15:5-7; Rom 7:12; 1Co 11:31-32; Eph 4:31-32, 5:1-3, 6:3; Php 4:3-4; 1Th 2:2-4; 2Ti 3:14-17; Heb 5:11-14; Jde 1:16-25; Rev 22:13-17.

Haven't I Seen You Here Before?

Hello! Haven't I seen you here before?
Haven't I heard you knocking at my door?
Look. Open the Book.
It's the Holy Bible. God's Holy Word.
Haven't you heard?
Listen. It's calling you.
It's telling you how to live the good life
without anger, contention, or strife.

It's telling you how to live without guilt.
How to eat the meat and wean yourself from the milk.
It's telling you to eat the honey—now, isn't that funny!
You can still have sweets for the sweet, but
you can no longer be drinking from the teat.

Before you know it, your hair will be turning gray.
What do you say?
It's time to grow up now.
You'll find what you need written in the Book.
Just look. It tells you how.
Here's a passage: Proverbs, Chapters 1-10.
Take a peek. It's there you'll find
the wisdom that you seek.

There are many other passages, too.
Here's one. It says why your eyes are so red.
It's because you "tarry too long at the wine."
Instead, the Bible says don't do that,
for in time it will "bite like a serpent
and sting like an adder."[1]
This is why your life continues on—
sadder and sadder.

See, I told you I've seen you here before.
Mark my words,
without penitence and remorse,
and without changing your course,
you will be here tomorrow,
with a heart still filled with pain,
trouble, and sorrow.

(Continued)

Hey you, sitting on the couch over there.
While drinking all that wine,
and resting on an incline.
Didn't you take a wife that wasn't thine?
The Word has a lot to say about that one.
But, you say, the less said the better.

So, what would you have me say?
That the Bible is a little old-fashioned?
It can't take into account the fiery passion
of an ardent young man like yourself?

Should Nathan have turned the other way,
so as not to betray
the fact David had sinned against God
when he took Bathsheba from her husband?
What then of David?
This mighty man—the King of Jerusalem?
Was he above the holy covenants and the law?

Heaven forbid! David was lost
when he forgot the Lord was Boss
and disobeyed His Commander.
In the end, it was Nathan's parable
that brought him around.

The story has since been told
over and over with renown.
"King, sir," he said, "What to do with the rich young ruler
who had a hundred sheep to slaughter,
but, instead stole, then cooked the single pet ewe lamb
owned by the poor old man?"

"What to do?" King David cried, fit to be tied.
"Hang him high. He must die. I will have no mercy!"
"Oh, but you see, my Lord," Nathan coolly replied.
"That man is *you*."

You know the story.
At that, King David immediately repented before God,
and he was given the nod
for both mercy and forgiveness.
He went down on his face
and was pardoned through grace,
but not before he had paid a consequence most grievous.

These are the sins that warp men's souls.
Too much wine combined with promiscuous women.
What to do? What *not* to do?
It's all written line by line
in the pages of time.

Yes, my son,
I have seen you here before,
I have heard you knocking at my door.
You and a hundredfold or more.

Those who continue on singing the lost man's song
will never belong in the Lamb's Book of Life.
Read what's there in the Holy Word.
It's a lot different than what you've heard
from Hollywood.

My son, I did not come to condemn you.
I came to save you from yourself.
Hear My Word.
It is holy, just, and good.
In it you will find salvation
with life eternal.

Come, sit here by Me,
beside the still waters
and rest your weary soul.

Obey my word.
Abide in Me, and I will be in Thee.
Then, you will see.

My plan has always been for you
to live long and prosper.
"Lo, I am with you always,
even unto the end of the world." [2]

1. Pro 23:30, 32; 2. Mat 28:20.

...beloved...keep yourselves in the love of God, looking for the mercy of our Lord Jesus Christ unto eternal life. And of some have compassion, making a difference: And others save with fear, pulling them out of the fire; hating even the garment spotted by the flesh. (Jde 1:21-23)

When our children are grown, we can't always prevent them from making poor life decisions. There are, however, several things we can do. We can give them good counsel if they ask and sometimes even if they don't. We can provide them with Bible passages that address their particular issues. And, last, all along the way, we can try to be the best example that we can so they can learn not only from what we say, but also from how we live our lives.

All this said, however, their potential for making right choices begins in the cradle. What our children do in their adult lives usually is a reflection on how they were raised from the time they were born. The Bible tells us to "train up a child in the way he should go; and when he is old, he will not depart from it." (Pro 22:6). I don't think anyone ever gave me advice any better than that. It certainly has proven true with my two sons. Sure, your child may stray from the straight and narrow at times, but he will eventually get back on course again—if you have given him the map and he knows the right way.

Along with all this is one other very important thing we need to remember to do and that is to pray for our children. My mother always said that worry never resolved anything, but prayer always gets results. Yes, the Lord does answer prayer, and we need to keep our children before Him every day in prayer—even when everything is going good.

Bible Study: Gen 14:18; Psa 30:9, 46:4, 57:2, 40:2, 103:3-5; Joh 14:6; Php 4:8; 1Th 4:16; Heb 11:1-3; 1Pe 3:21; Jde:1:1-25; Rev 15:3.

From the Parent to the Child:
Contending for the Faith

This vow I pledge, I pledge not just to you,
but to our Most High and Holy God,
the One Who's Just and True.
This is the promise that I cry:
"Christ will not let you down nor I."

With a touch from the One Who saves,
we lift our hearts to Him in praise,
confirming together you will not slip
into that dark, seductive pit—
to be forever lost in sin,
held captive by the arms of
Satan's men.

And, when that trump of God will sound,
your feet then firm on Holy Ground,
we as contenders of the faith,
will hold steadfast with clasping hands,
and in Christ's love forever stand.

The day is thine, the night also is thine: thou hast prepared the light and the sun. (Psa 74:16)

I wrote this poem one night when I had insomnia. It is in such moments of solitude when I feel closest to the Lord. Sitting in my recliner, I continued writing into the early hours of morning, occasionally stopping to gaze out my living room window as the blackness of the sky gradually morphed into the blue light of morning. With my writing completed, I watched Venus, the last star left in the brightening sky fade into a most spectacular sunrise that lit up the eastern horizon.

At that moment, a peace flowed over my spirit as I thought of the correlation between the morning sun and Christ. Yes, we can have even more confidence in Christ than we can in the sun coming up. As that old song says: "The sun'll come out tomorrow, bet your bottom dollar that tomorrow there'll be sun..." [1] In the same way, Christ is always with us and will be there for us always and some day He will return. You can "bet your bottom dollar" on that, too!

To old family friends,
Pat Noonan and children, Jacob and Carlie,
George Hubmaeir, Charlie Morris, and Ed Geimer,
and our "newer" friends, Dr. Harpreet Jaswal, Sherri Hemminger,
Rick Ingalsbe, Preston Kabinoff, and Richard Lindstrom

Tell them [your friends] *how great things the Lord hath done for thee...* (Mar 5:19)

1. Song, *Tomorrow* from musical, *Annie:* Music by Charles Strouse and lyrics by Martin Charnin, 1977.

Bible Study: Psa 24:6-10; Isa 7:14, 9:2, 6-7; Mat 28:6-7; Mar 16:2-6; Luk 24:1-10; Joh 5:25-32, 11:25, 20:1-21, 21:14; Act 1:22, 2:31, 4:33; Rom 8:34; 1Co 15:1-3, 54-58; Rev 1:1-19, 22:12-18.

Transcendence: Out of Darkness

As the black, starry sky gives way
at break of day to dawn's first light,
the sun in its habitual rising gives blessed assurance—
Day does follow Night.

At that moment, high in the Eastern sky,
against a backdrop of dusky blue,
only the brilliance of one solitary star remains.

For this freshly awakened world,
the Star's singular splendor
is an everlasting witness to the coming Light—
the Light once thought was lost forever in sleeping darkness.

In that shadowy place where dreams are born in blackness,
where all are blind, but some can see with spiritual eyes only,
our souls were unwittingly locked in an internal, infernal battle
between heavenly angels and devilish dragons.

Then, the Cross at Calvary changed everything.
There, in a realm unseen,
in a paradox of sweet dreams and acrid nightmares,
God's Goodness overcame Satan's Evil in one moment of time,
for the salvation of an errant, sin-filled mankind.

Now, as Night gives way to Light,
and the familiar, golden orb begins to ascend
once again into the blue, veiled hue,
we know, as sure as the morning sun,
the Lord does transcend it all.

Expectation

This We Can Be Sure Of...

His name shall endure for ever: his name shall be continued as long as the sun: and men shall be blessed in him: all nations shall call him blessed... Blessed be the Lord God, the God of Israel, who only doeth wondrous things. And blessed be his glorious name for ever: and let the whole earth be filled with his glory. (Psa 72:17-19)

* * *

Now unto him that is able to keep you from falling, and to present you faultless before the presence of his glory with exceeding joy, to the only wise God our Saviour, be glory and majesty, dominion and power, both now and ever. Amen. (Jde 1:24-25)

"Let Go and Let God"
and Other Tried and True Clichés

Commit thy way unto the Lord; trust also in him; and he shall bring it to pass. (Psa 37:5)

No matter how strong we are as Christians, each of us has in the past and will in the future go through periods of harsh trial and testing. The Lord said the rain falls "on the just and on the unjust" (Mat 5:45). Sometimes it can get so bad we want to shout: "Lord, I can't take it any more!" The fact is things happen in life we can't control, no matter how much we prepare. Sometimes good things happen. Sometimes bad things happen. Even worse, quite a bit of the bad things in life happen to us because of our own actions.

My mother was the queen of the old tried and true clichés. She used to say: "The Lord gives each of us our own cross to bear." She also taught me with that cross, He gives us a way through it. Yes, it is very clichéd, but it's so true. I've found it to be so over and over again in my life. When things were at their worst, my mother would say, "We just have to hunker down in this storm and go through the rough waters until the bad times subside." In other words: "Deal with it." Yep, that's another good cliché for us all to remember. But, how do we do that? For sure, it's not always an easy thing. My mother had another favorite one for that, too. She would say: "Let go and let God."

In Philippians, Paul laid out an action plan to "let go and let God." He tells us:

> ...this one thing I do, forgetting those things which are behind, and reaching forth unto those things which are before, I press toward the mark for the prize of the high calling of God in Christ Jesus. Let us therefore, as many as be perfect [complete], be thus minded: and if in any thing ye be otherwise minded, God shall reveal even this unto you. (Php 3:13-14).

If you know the story of Paul, you know he went through shipwrecks, beatings, and imprisonment—all for his faithful following of Christ. But, before he met Jesus, Paul had been a Pharisee who was responsible for the deaths of many Christian believers, including the angelic Stephen (Act 7). At times, his guilt overwhelmed him. But, as he said, he "pressed on."

Paul is a great example of being an "overcomer." As a follower of Christ, he had to overcome obstacles and persecutions, but first he had to overcome his own guilt for the lifestyle he had lived before he came to know Christ. Paul tells us over and over in his writings that he could do this only through the indwelling of the Holy Spirit and through his faith in the Lord Jesus Christ.

So, what is Paul telling us here in this passage? He is literally laying out his action plan for us. First, he says to "forget those things which are behind." Paul is basically saying, using my mother's tried and true clichés: "Don't cry over spilt milk." "What's done is done and can't be undone." "The past is past." "What's writ is writ." In other words, you can't change what has already occurred. What you can do is learn from your mistakes and repent of those mistakes when necessary. Then, ask the Lord's forgiveness. Finally, move on from there.

Next, Paul says he reaches "forth unto those things which are before." Notice he uses the word "reach." Again, this has to do with "action." After we have put the past behind us, we are to start consciously and with great effort to "press toward the mark [the goal] for the prize of the high calling of God in Christ Jesus." In other words, Paul wants us to set our goals into action along with a specific plan to accomplish those goals. These goals, he says, involve "pressing" forward and toward something—something much bigger than ourselves, something that may seem unattainable to some, but not to Paul and not to us as Christians. That goal is the "high calling of God in Christ Jesus."

For us, that "high calling" Paul is talking about here is the will of Christ in our lives, and it is something different and unique for each and every one of us. Even more importantly, as we set our own action plan and goals into place, we cannot necessarily know what that "high calling" will be in our lives. We just have to move in the direction that the Lord sets for us by trusting and obeying Him with our whole heart. The Bible tells us that the Lord will "direct our paths" and that we should not "lean unto our own understanding" (Pro 3:5-6). And, how do we accomplish this? As my mother would say: "Baby step by baby step" on a daily basis—"just like the turtle, slowly but surely." And, in order to obey the Lord, we need to get into the habit of reading our Bibles daily and setting aside a quiet time for prayer and meditation, for these are the building blocks to knowing the right path to follow.

Along the way, we'll get off track now and then. When we do, we have to reset, repent, and start anew, always pressing toward that beautiful true and perfect "mark" that the Lord has set for us. Just remember what my mother would say: "Rome wasn't built in a day." "You have to walk before you can run." "A thousand-mile journey begins with just one step."

For sure, the goal Paul is talking about in his letter to the Philippians is a much higher goal than any we would set for ourselves. It's also a mark the world will tell us is impossible to reach. And, it would be impossible to attain if left to ourselves. But, Paul says, this prize is "in Christ Jesus," and we know from another passage by Paul in Philippians that we "can do all things through Christ which strengthens [us]" (Php 4:13). Jesus Himself tells us that "with God all things are possible" (Mar 10:27). So, despite all the odds and regardless our circumstances or our past, we can accomplish the goal the Lord sets before us. Even more importantly, by working towards that goal, we will change our mindset from thinking about all our failures to keeping our eye on the prize that is at the end when we reach our mark.

Paul ends this passage by saying that in doing this we should all be "thus minded" or "like-minded" unless God "reveals" something different to us. We read in Psalms:

> Trust in the LORD, and do good; so shalt thou dwell in the land, and verily thou shalt be fed. Delight thyself also in the LORD: and he shall give thee the desires of thine heart. Commit thy way unto the LORD; trust also in him; and he shall bring it to pass. (Psa 37:3-5)

In other words, we should all make our own individual action plans for the "high calling of God" by trusting and committing whatever we do in life to Him. We aren't to do this begrudgingly, the Psalm tells us. We are to do so with great enthusiasm and "delight." Best of all, there are rewards for our efforts. Not only will we be comfortable and well-fed, but we will also receive "the desires of our heart." Wow! It can't get any better than that! And, when should we get started? Well, as my mother would say: "There's no time like the present."

To my sister Barbara, with much affection and love,
and to all her family as well:
My nieces and nephews, Sharon, Eddie, B.J.,
David and his wife, Lisa, Melvin Jr. and his wife, Meagan,
Carrie, her daughter, Ashton, and all their families.

Finding God is a "heart" thing.
Follow Jesus and enjoy the journey.
He will show you the way.

Trust in the Lord with all thine heart... (Pro 3:5)

Then shall we know, if we follow on to know the LORD: his going forth is prepared as the morning; and he shall come unto us as the rain, as the latter [spring] and former [autumn] rain unto the earth. (Hos 6:3)

Sometimes the healing of our souls comes through moments in time like this one I experienced. We know it's only temporary, but it gets us through and gives us inner strength—until the next time.

In the Bible, the writers use a variety of nature attributes in describing the Lord. In the Old Testament Book of Hosea, the writer describes the Lord's appearing to be as certain as the "morning," i.e. the sun coming up. And, how will He come to us? Hosea says He will come as the rain, both the spring and the autumn rains, denoting both Christ's first and second comings.

The Bible tells us our Lord is that thirst-quenching, spiritual "eternal waters" that soak into every fiber of our being, bringing regeneration to both body and spirit. The cascading drive of His life-giving, life-sustaining power washes over our hearts and purifies the soul, bringing a comfort and peace that passes all understanding. Through each mystical, magical droplet of His divine rain, the miracle of a brand new life in the Spirit is nurtured and grows, creating in each saved soul a heavenly spirit that will live eternally after our physical bodies are long dead and buried.

To deny the thrust and magnitude of such an awesome, wondrous force is pure, unadulterated folly. If you haven't as yet accepted Jesus as your Lord and Savior, won't you come and be a part of His grand and glorious spiritual realm! Doing so will make all the difference in how you spend Eternity.

With love to the Vegluccis: Joe and Maria, Joey and Theresa.
You are our friends forever in Christ.

"Sometimes me think, 'What is friend?'
And then me say ... 'Friend is someone
to share the last cookie with.'"
—Cookie Monster (*Sesame Street*)

Bible Study: Gen 1:9-13; Deu 32:1-4; 2Sa 23:1-7; Psa 72:6; 16, 103:13-20, 147:7-8; Isa 40:5-8; Zec 10:1; Mat 6:30; 1Pe 1:24-25; Rev 9:4.

Soft Rain

A soft rain falls outside my window.
Its sounds play in consonance with
the steady rhythm of my heart.

I watch mesmerized as each liquid bead
bounces off budding greenery, flower petals, and
blades of freshly mown grass.

With a splatter, each bursts forth into tiny crystal rivulets,
randomly rushing headlong on their cursory course
to a pre-arranged destiny of final absorption.

Light rain. Latter rain. Spring rain.
It fills my soul. My cup overflows.
As quickly as it had begun,
this afternoon shower is almost done.

Comforting. Soothing. Relaxing.
This spring rain washes the earth and cleanses the heart,
leaving my inner being composed and serene.
Ever so gently, it lulls me into a welcoming nap.

I wake refreshed.
From my window, as I soak in the beauty
of a freshly bathed earth,
I see sunlight sparkling through silkened threads
of dwindling raindrops.
Renewed and invigorated, I stretch relaxed muscles and
breathe in ionic-charged air.

For the moment, peace prevails
deep within the recesses of my soul.
With it, tranquility is sustained,
like the vibrancy of green after the rain.

The grass withereth, the flower fadeth: but the word of our God shall stand for ever. (Isa 40:8)

In the Bible, the word, "virgin," is sometimes used as a metaphor for Christians, representing the "Virgin Birth." Flowers as well are sometimes used as a symbol for God's holy children who grow among the "grass," with the "grass" representing all the peoples of the world. In reality, the flowers themselves are simply "blooming" grass. All grow together in the light of the sun, with the bright flowers bringing a colorful splash and diverse beauty to the one-dimensional green of the field. Sadly, all will eventually fade and die, quickly perishing—even the flowers in their full, glorious array. Such is the circle of life. But, the Good News is that this life isn't all there is. As Christians, we've been given the promise of eternal life in the Son, Jesus Christ.

This poem was written during a time when I was very ill, right before a major surgery. It was a surgery that would take a long time to heal. After a pity party of one, with me crying, "Why me Lord?" I finally stopped and looked at my surroundings. In the midst of my anxiety, the Lord suddenly gave me peace and quietness in my spirit. My surgery was out of town. My two wonderful sons had made reservations for my husband and me at a quaint, historical southern Bed and Breakfast just around the corner from the hospital. Our little suite even had a whirlpool bath and a colorful garden out back.

I didn't know what the morrow would bring, but at that moment, I decided to enjoy the pleasant atmosphere our sons had provided for this time prior to surgery. I took a long, leisurely bath in the whirlpool tub, dressed, and went out and sat in the garden for a while reading my Bible. Then, I ordered a nice takeout dinner for two from a highly recommended restaurant, and my husband and I enjoyed the rest of the evening. That night before I fell asleep, I wrote this poem, acknowledging the source of all my comfort, mercy, and strength. Before I drifted off, I prayed to the Lord to see me through those difficult and painful circumstances, and He did. That was almost 20 years ago.

There are so many things that give us doubt, including pain, suffering, sickness and disease. Yet, we can know with a certainty we will all be together again with Christ and live forever in Heaven if we accept Him as our Lord and Savior. As Christians, Jesus never promised we wouldn't face tribulation in this world, but He did promise He would be there with us—all the way to the end and beyond. He has proven that to me time and again.

Bible Study: Exo 25:21; Num 8:4; 1Ki 6:32, 7:49; Psa 103:15; Sos 2:12; Isa 7:14, 40:6-8, 62:5; Jer 31:4,13, 21; Mat 1:23, 25:1-13; Luk 1:27; 1Co 7:34; 2Co 11:2; Jam 1:10; 1Pe 1:24; Rev 14:4.

Eternal Spring

The daisy petals are plucked
by a fair young maiden
and fall one by one
on life's dewy grass of green.
"He loves me—He loves me not,"
is the beloved Virgin's earthly refrain.

But, when the grassy slopes of life
have faded into billowy clouds of white,
and all that be around us 'bout
is a lustrous, brilliant Light.

There'll be no more doubts,
laments, regrets, or sorrow—
only Eternal Spring,
and the joyous song we sing of everything
will be to our Savior, Lord, and King.

Jesus loves me, this I know[1]*—*
Oh, how He loves me,
Oh, how He loves you,
Oh, how He loves you and me.[2]

1. Excerpt from the Song: *Jesus Loves Me* by Anna B. Warner, 1860,
   with added lyrics by David Rutherford McGuire, 1862.

2. Excerpt from the Song: *Oh, How He Loves You and Me* by Kurt Kaiser, 1975.

...we look not at the things which are seen, but at the things which are not seen: for the things which are seen are temporal; but the things which are not seen are eternal. (2Co 4:18)

I was almost asleep one night when this poem came to me. Immediately, I got up and wrote out the basic theme—life at a glance, from youth through old age with a Christian perspective. In narrative form, it's quite different from most of the poems I've written.

The inspiration was a pleasant old man my husband and I saw one day sitting on our rock wall. That particular day we could see the dim, faint moon high in the blue afternoon sky. The old gentleman was sitting there looking up at it trying to catch his breath. We enquired if we could help him in any way, but he said "No." He just wanted to visit this place where he used to hike as a youth. We then gave him his privacy and left him to his reminiscing. This visual was so vivid that it had stayed with me. Then, one night, the idea of this poem came to me. I sketched it out and went back to sleep. In the following days, I reworked my ideas, making the narrator a young man and putting in a few twists here and there. Finally my little parable was done.

In this poem, we watch as the narrator journeys through his life at warp speed. You might say he meets himself coming and going. It's not the events or the journey itself at the forefront, but the realization of how fast this temporal life can pass us by. We've all heard the expression: "Life is not a destination, but a journey." Neither is the "End Game" of life a destination, as some people would have us believe. Instead, it is the beginning of an excursion into eternity. In order to know where we're going on that excursion, however, we first need to meet the one who will take us there. His name is Jesus Christ of Nazareth. He paid our passage ahead of time by way of the Cross at Calvary, and He has all the provisions we'll need for our trip.

Are you prepared for your eternal sojourn? Are you sure you've booked the "right" passage? Do you know Jesus? If not, won't you get to know Him this day? At the end, wouldn't you like to hear Him say: "Welcome to Heaven. We know you will enjoy your stay."

To Ian and Libby (Mary) with love:
Our friends in Christ and "cruising buddies."
Fifty years of friendship and counting.
And to our new cruising buddies, too:
Nick & Ella and Ernie & Alice.
You're all "platinum!"

Friends are like stars...you may not always see them,
but you know they are there.—Anon.

Bible Study: Gen 15:15; Exo 33:22; Lev 19:32; Num 20:8; Deu 32:4; 1Sa 2:2; Psa 8:3-4, 18:2, 31-46, 27:5, 28:1, 31:3, 42:9, 61:2, 62:2-7, 71:3, 72:5-7, 78:35, 89:26-37, 90:10, 94:22, 95:1, 104:19; Pro 16:31, 25:25; Ecc 3:3, 7:1; Isa 46:4; Mat 7:24, 25:14; Luk 19:12; Rom 14:8; 1Co 10:4, 15:42-44.

Rite of Passage:
An Old Man and the Moon

And even to your old age I am he; and even to hoar [gray] hairs will I carry you:
I have made, and I will bear; even I will carry, and will deliver you. (Isa 46:4)

One evening, as I was out walking,
I saw an old man sitting on a rock
looking at the moon.
His wide-brimmed hat sat back on his head, and
his chiseled face was set in a smile framed with wrinkles.

"Old man," said I,
"Don't you have better things to do with your time
than just sit there on that rock looking at the moon?"
He gazed up at me and widening his smile, he replied:
"What better place to meet my Maker
than sitting on this rock enjoying the Nature He created?

There's a time to be born. There's a time to die.
There's a time to laugh. There's a time to cry. [1]
You still have lots of work to do.
Your time will come. Pass on by."

And, that's exactly what I did.
After I had gone quite a distance, though,
I turned to see if he was still there.
He was gone, but there on the rock was his hat.
I went back and picked it up.
Inside the rim was embroidered his name: "Christian."

That was strange. That was my name, too.
I placed the hat on my head,
sat on the rock,
and looked up at the moon.

I found the old man was right.
There had never been a finer site than this
to sit and to contemplate all God's creation, and
to thank Him for all He had given—
including His blessings, His mercies, His grace,
and eternal life in Heaven.

(Continued)

For quite a while,
I continued to sit on the rock looking at the moon.
While I was contemplating and meditating,
I could see the beginning of a great bright light.
But, in the middle of my reverie, I was interrupted.
There in front of me stood a young man.

Somehow I knew what he was going to say.
He didn't even begin with "Good day."
"Old man," said he, "Should you be
just sitting there on a rock looking at the moon?
You know, you're going to die soon."

"Yes, son, I suppose I will.
You might be surprised, though,
how soon you might want to join me.
But, for now, be on your way.
I'll just continue to stay here on this rock and pray,
looking at the moon and considering the works of God
and all His wonders under Heaven."

Then, I blinked and the young man was gone.
But, instead of sitting on a rock looking at the moon,
I found myself in a different place—in a quiet space.
It was that glorious far country out beyond the stars,
and all around me was the presence of God.

1. Ecc 3:2, 4.

Blessed Assurance

From Death Unto Life...

Moreover, brethren, I declare unto you the gospel which I preached unto you, which also ye have received, and wherein ye stand; By which also ye are saved, if ye keep in memory what I preached unto you...how that Christ died for our sins according to the scriptures; And that he was buried, and that he rose again the third day according to the scriptures...

For as in Adam all die, even so in Christ shall all be made alive. But every man in his own order: Christ the firstfruits; afterward they that are Christ's at his coming. Then cometh the end, when he shall have delivered up the kingdom to God, even the Father; when he shall have put down all rule and all authority and power. For he must reign, till he hath put all enemies under his feet. The last enemy that shall be destroyed is death.

And so it is written, The first man Adam was made a living soul; the last Adam was made a quickening spirit...The first man is of the earth, earthy; the second man is the Lord from heaven...And as we have borne the image of the earthy, we shall also bear the image of the heavenly.

So when this corruptible shall have put on incorruption, and this mortal shall have put on immortality, then shall be brought to pass the saying that is written, Death is swallowed up in victory. O death, where is thy sting? O grave, where is thy victory? The sting of death is sin; and the strength of sin is the law. But thanks be to God, which giveth us the victory through our Lord Jesus Christ. (1Co 15: 1-4, 22-26, 45, 47, 49, 54-57)

Elmwood Cemetery

And unto this people thou shalt say, Thus saith the Lord; Behold, I set before you the way of life, and the way of death. (Jer 21:8)

It's an old Southern custom during the holidays to visit the gravesites of relatives and loved ones past. On my mother's side of the family, this was a regular tradition. Around Easter, she would pack the four of us children in the family automobile. Along with my aunts, uncles, and cousins, we would form a caravan of cars to visit Grandmother Carrie's grave at Elmwood Cemetery. My father, however, would always find a way to avoid these annual pilgrimages.

By the time I was six, my two older siblings had left home, leaving just my brother, Greg, and me to accompany my mother. The year I was ten, we weren't able to have the typical large family gathering. My mother, however, still felt it necessary for someone to go with us. That year she invited my father's Aunt Pansy.

In the early afternoon, my aunt and her three grandchildren—Jackie, Joe, and Jim—arrived at our house with a full picnic basket, including pimento cheese sandwiches, sliced watermelon, and fresh peaches. Mama added some ham sandwiches, potato salad, store-bought Hostess cupcakes, and a large insulated jug of iced tea. With blankets and a full supply of food, we all piled into the family car and off we went.

Once there and settled in, Mama and Aunt Pansy attended to the gravesite, removing old flowers, cleaning up, and arranging new bouquets. They also used this time to relax and visit while all us "young-uns" wandered off to explore the graveyard, making sure we followed proper protocol by walking *around* and not *over* the graves.

Absorbed in reading gravestones and playing "chase," the five of us quickly lost track of where we were. Finally taking time to rest, we realized we were far beyond Grandma's gravesite. In fact, we had reached an area where the grounds were no longer maintained. From here on, the grass was tall and full of weeds.

We were about to turn back when the oldest, Jackie, suggested we find the fence where the graveyard ended. It seemed a good idea, so we ventured on. Once through the tangled weeds, however, instead of a fence we suddenly found ourselves in the midst of an old Civil War-era graveyard. There before us was a small plot of hand-chiseled, roughly-hewn rectangular stone grave markers. Some were so worn we couldn't read the now-faded words.

Upon realizing what the names, dates, and dedications meant, we ran back to announce our discovery. Mama and Aunt Pansy were quickly caught up in our enthusiasm and came back with us to explore the old graves.

Later, as everyone else was returning to my grandmother's graveside, I stopped at the top of a hill to take in a deep breath. It was so peaceful that I lingered there a while to enjoy this solitary moment. I found a comfortable spot and stretched out on the soft grass. A gentle breeze stirred, rustling the leaves above as it cooled my warm, damp skin.

Even for a child, there is something very sobering about viewing the final resting place of those who have gone before. In my youthful imagination, I envisioned these illusive souls clasping hand in hand across the corridors of history.

My thoughts were suddenly interrupted by someone calling my name. I looked up. It was my cousin, Jim.

"Come on, Slowpoke!" he yelled. "We thought you were lost."

"No, just resting!" I yelled back.

With that, I jumped up and walked towards him. When I got closer, I quipped: "Bet I can beat you back!"

At that, I tagged him and started running. He took the challenge and darted after me. I could feel him close behind, but I couldn't look back for fear of stepping on a grave. Our race ended in a tie. Laughing and out of breath, we rejoined the group.

That lazy spring afternoon, the five of us youngsters frolicked and pranced among the gravestones like playful yearlings in an open field. From mid-afternoon to dusk, we whiled away the hours, searching out names and dates among a historical treasure trove of headstones. In between, we played childish games of "chase" and "hide-and-seek." Though respectful of where we stepped, we were still quite oblivious to the actual physical remains that lay just beneath our feet.

In the cemetery that day in our youthful naïveté, we could not as yet appreciate the full impact of these departed souls with their eulogies etched on a plethora of granite stones. Nor could we fathom the role they had once played during their earthly existence or how it all related to our present day.

Indeed, we could no more understand how we had benefited in our own lives from the fruits of their long-forgotten labors than we could comprehend how the withered, decaying leaves of autumns past had nurtured the existence of the verdant, young leaves now extending high above us in the towering elms.

Just the same, the connection was there, for the crumpled, decaying vegetation at our feet not only sustained life, but was also vital to bringing vibrant *new* life into the world. Those seemingly dead leaves at the bottom of these trees were in fact responsible in great measure for how high the spry new leaves would soar.

In a similar fashion, the departed souls resting in this serene cemetery had once existed in the same place where we now stood. They had all contributed in various ways to our present generation's security, well-being, and vitality. Both individually and collectively, their endeavors afforded us the opportunity to live and be nurtured in safe surroundings. This, in turn, would help us grow and mature to our full potential.

With the simple placement of dates and brief eulogies, these tombstones told an abbreviated tale of birth through death. Some lives had been cut short by accident, disease, or war. But, the vast majority had lived a full life and had not "shuffled off this mortal coil"[1] until they were bent and aged and had donned hoary, gray heads, with deep lines chiseled in once smooth faces.

While still alive, they had dreams and ambitions. They, too, shared similar emotions that we the living were now experiencing. They felt love and desire, set life goals, experienced joy and despair, laughter and tears, painful suffering, and wholesome wonderment. They savored the spring air filled with the fresh fragrance of honeysuckle and jasmine, felt the change of summer's heat to autumn's cooling chill, and endured the shivery blast of a wintry wind.

Regardless of when and how they died, these souls had all completed their trek on this earth and then passed on—some to eternal glory and others to an unfathomable damnation.

There among the gravestones on that day so many years ago, I had no fear or trepidation of being in such a hallowed place. Even in the innocence of my youth, I knew the basic theological truth regarding the spiritual realm. There were no ghosts or tormented souls of the dearly departed still lingering under the tall elms that covered the cemetery landscape—nor had there ever been.

For sure, we would find no such spirits floating among the Spanish moss or reclining on the tombstones such as those depicted in cartoons and movies. No, the spirits of these dead had long since left their bodies—and this earth—to points known only by the Creator of it all.

According to the Bible, after death there is only a vital impression of one's spirit left in its former surroundings—and *not* the spirit itself. When we die and the vessel that is our body is broken, our spirit returns to the Lord—the One Who made us in the first place (Ecc 12:7). All that remains of those who passed on are memories—reflections, images, and impressions captured in our minds or in writings, photos, and videos.

Jesus Himself tells us the spirits of the departed cannot come back to "guide us" or to "haunt us" (Luk 16:19-31). In other words, there is no such thing as communication with the dead. This we can know for certain through the reading of God's Word.

Christian souls rest peacefully in the cradle of the Lord until His Second Coming (1Th 4:14; 5:10; 1Co 15:51). In contrast, the unsaved return to the dust of shadows and unrest while awaiting final judgment (Dan 12:2; Luk 16:20-31).

That said, I have it on good authority from some in the older generation—but it is only conjecture, mind you—that our dearly departed, as they leave this earth for their final destination, can sometimes indicate their passing with unexplained footsteps, a flickering light, or some other physical sign. Such happenings would not necessarily be out of keeping with the Bible's teachings.

Indeed, there are many things regarding death we cannot know for sure, for the Bible reveals only what we need to know in the here and now. The Apostle Paul put it this way: "We now see through a glass darkly..." (1Co 3:12). That pretty much sums it up.

In this life, we remain mostly "in the dark" on such spiritual matters. As followers of Christ, however, we know that death is not the end. Indeed, it is but the *beginning* of life eternal. As Christians, we can be assured that, in passing, we will go to be with our Lord and Savior in Heaven forever (Joh 3:16-17).

The Bible tells us we will see our Christian loved ones once again in the "Great By and By." For sure, we are not saying good-bye forever to the departed, but only "So long" for a little while. At the time of their passing, this can provide great comfort. It is all part of the "blessed assurance" we have as Christians regarding life after death (Heb 11:16; Rev 7:9-17).

Paul also said we will be transformed from the physical into the spiritual. We will go from being a finite, temporal entity with both a body and spirit to one that is entirely spiritual and yet has a bodily *appearance*. This is a mystery, but, at the time of the Rapture, this transformation will occur "...in a moment, in a twinkling of an eye" (1Co 15:52). In other words, it will be immediate.

The Apostle John tells us that after Christ's return, we will all live with Him in a place of abundance and beauty. There we will find splendid lodgings in a beautiful garden overflowing with the fruit of eternal life (1Jo 2:25). The river of life will be running through it (Rev 22:1-2). And, in the midst of this Paradise, there will be a sparkling silver fountain of everlasting waters (Rev 7:17). In this place—in the center of this "Garden" of perfect peace called "The City of God" (Rev 3:12)—we will all sup together with our Lord around a table that is filled with His wonderful Grace (Rev 19:9).

This is not fable, fantasy, or fiction. It is the glorious reality of knowing, accepting, and believing in our Lord and Savior Jesus Christ.

1. William Shakespeare, *Hamlet*, Act 3, scene i.

For God so loved the world, that he gave his only begotten Son, that whosoever believeth in him should not perish, but have everlasting life. (Joh 3:16)

This poem was written as a memorial for my brother-in-law, Robert J. Salvesen, a fine Christian man and beloved family member who had served in the Navy during WWII. He loved the ocean. After he retired from law, he and his wife, Ginger, moved to a seaside condo in Lincoln City, Oregon. One of Bob's favorite poems was "Sea Fever" by John Masefield, Poet Laureate of England. I started my poem with part of a line from that work and carried it through using a similar rhythm and cadence, with the theme of everlasting life.

The good news for Christians is that we know this life is not all there is. There is so much more awaiting us on the other side in glory. We can have hope through Christ's Resurrection and confidence in His merciful grace that we will live with Him forever in Heaven. We know, too, when our Christian family and friends pass on, they go to a much better place and that we will join them one day. There is such great comfort in knowing this.

In Loving Memory:

Robert J. Salvesen

January 2, 1922 ✝ October 10, 2000

Bible Study: Gen 1:10, 22, 26, 22:17, 32:12, 49:13; Psa 24:2, 33:7, 65:5, 69:34, 72:8, 74:13, 78:53, 89:25; Zec 9:10; Mat 4:1, 13, 15, 18, 24, 26-27, 13:11, 41; Mar 14:25-29, 17:27; Rev 4:6, 5:13, 22:17.

To the Sea Again

I must go down to the sea again
to set sail in the mist and the foam.
I must go down to the sea again,
my soul has been called home.

The anchor's aweigh.
My course is set.
My Master has now released me.

But, don't cry, my Pet.
Don't cry, my friends,
for my fate is not the sea.

When you go down to the sea again,
look out on that vast horizon.
You'll know I'm not gone
nor all alone.
I am where I long to be.

I've found my rest
in the arms of the Son
for all Eternity.

Who can find a virtuous woman? for her price is far above rubies…Strength and honour are her clothing; and she shall rejoice in time to come…Her children arise up, and call her blessed; her husband also, and he praiseth her. Many daughters have done virtuously, but thou excellest them all. (Pro 31:10, 25, 28-29)

My mother was truly a blessed lady and fits this well-known Bible passage to a "T." She instilled in me a love of Jesus and encouraged me to be my "own person" and to never compromise my beliefs. She was the epitome of a true Christian with strong spiritual values and a tenderness and graciousness beyond compare.

This very important lady also gave me an appreciation for all things both practical and fun, including music and dancing. She taught me to enjoy life no matter the circumstances and that, sometimes, we all should just "let loose" and dance to the music. This poem is for the sweetest lady I ever knew—my Mom.

In memory of my mother,
with the greatest love and affection:

Elmarrine Roberts Bullard
April 28, 1918 ✝ January 5, 2002

Bible Study: Exo 15:20; 1Sa 29:5; 2Sa 6:14; Job 21:11; Psa 149:3, 150:4; Pro 31:10, 25, 28-29; Ecc 3:4; Jer 31:4, 13; Rev 22:14.

Carolina Child

A Carolina baby.
A Carolina child.
The favored of God's children,
Mama has a Carolina smile.

Rocked gently in the cradle.
Raised in whispering pines.
She sang those sweet songs of Jesus,
through life's good and bad times.

Dancing in the twilight,
laughing in the rain,
Mama taught her children well,
echoing the love of Jesus
in her own sweet life's refrain.

She's our Carolina darlin'.
She's our Carolina pride.
She's our Carolina sweetheart.
But, she's sweet Jesus' bride.

Rock the cradle gently.
Croon the songs awhile.
Mama's comin', Jesus—
She's *your* Carolina child.

But as for you, teach what accords with sound doctrine. Older men are to be sober-minded, dignified, self-controlled, sound in faith, in love, and in steadfastness. (Tit 2:1-2 ESV)

...publish ye, praise ye, and say, O LORD, save thy people, the remnant of Israel. (Jer 31:7)

This particular poem was written by my late father. He was both a writer and an artist. I am publishing it here as a tribute to him.

From the time I was a little girl, my father instilled in me a sincere empathy and concern for others, the desire to attain to the highest moral standards, and the courage to take chances in life. Early on, he gave me a sense of adventure and a love of books. In the process, he encouraged my storytelling and writing. He inspired me to follow my dreams and to set my sights on achieving my goals.

Though he didn't find the Lord until late in life, the book Daddy and I read the most together was the Holy Bible. He continually challenged me to study the Word and to know why I believed in the Lord Jesus Christ. Ironically, he followed the tenets of the faith long before I was born. And yet, he was close to death before he finally accepted the Lord into his heart.

Daddy wrote this poem when he first realized he was gravely ill. At the time, no one in the family knew. I didn't understand until years later that this poem was about death—*his* death. He told me then that his writings were mostly historical narratives that were quite impersonal. Daddy went on to say there was "heart" and "depth" in my writings that he very much appreciated. He also was impressed with my use of symbolism. This poem, he said, was his effort to do the same. I felt so complimented that I gave him a big hug!

About a year after this was written, he was on his deathbed. My uncle Elmer phoned long distance to say Daddy had finally accepted Jesus as His Lord and Savior. We had all been praying so long for this! My father had taken my uncle's hand and whispered: "Do I have to be baptized to come on profession of faith? I want to do it now. Is it too late?"

My uncle replied: "No, David, it's not too late." Then, he took out the Bible and read the appropriate words, dipping water from the bedside pitcher and baptizing my father in the name of the Father, Son, and Holy Spirit. That day, my mother, Uncle Elmer, Aunt Mag, and I all rejoiced together over the telephone. We knew my father would soon be with the Lord. Less than two weeks later, he died. It had been a long journey for him, but he made it, and now he is in the arms of Jesus.

In memory of my father,
with the greatest love and affection:

David Franklin Bullard
December 16, 1913 ✞ November 21, 1981

Bible Study: Psa 13:5, 45:1, 62:1; Jer 31:7; Luk 23:43; Heb 2:3; Jud 1:3; Rev 19:1.

The Last Burning Ember

The extended hand hesitates
to toss a tot of icy cold water
on the last burning ember,
the last burning ember of the fire.

The fire that had warmed them,
the fire that had held
the menacing predators to a distance
from the camp through the night.

The fire that had provided heat to make
edible the food that would otherwise
be returned to earth to nourish root or mouth
first to chance on such good fortune.

But still, the halting hand hesitates
to tilt the cup as the glowing ember fades.
Now! The hand is forced
and the deed is done.

Yes, the deed is done—to a sizzling cackle
of steaming resentment,
but the deed is done, and a tear is shed
for the *last burning ember*.

Train up a child in the way he should go: and when he is old, he will not depart from it. (Pro 22:6)...Remember now thy Creator in the days of thy youth...Then shall the dust return to the earth as it was: and the spirit shall return unto God who gave it. (Ecc 12:1, 7)

This poem was written as a memorial for my 20-year-old great nephew, Michael. His life had been in flux, and he was finding his way. Yes, he had stumbled quite a bit, but he was on the right path. He had accepted the Lord as his personal Savior and was in the midst of "working out his own salvation" (Php 2:12-13) when he died unexpectedly. The Good News is that he knew the Lord.

Our children become a vital part of us from the moment of conception. We cherish them and do our best to protect them and keep them from harm. They are our reason for living, our lifeline and joy in youth, and our comfort in old age. Our children are supposed to outlive us. To lose a child is the worst kind of suffering one can bear.

When it happens, it is devastating, and there appears to be no comfort, no solace, no consolation for the pain of so great a loss. But, there is. It can be found in Christ Jesus. God the Father went through this agony when His only Son took up the Cross to die for the sins of all mankind. The Father allowed Jesus to go through this ordeal so those who would believe in Christ and follow Him could have eternal life in Heaven.

We can never know why such tragedy happens, but through Christ's suffering on the Cross, we can know without a doubt that our God is not a distant God Who would leave us to our own devices here on this earth. He suffers with us as well as suffered for us and lifts us up in the time of our most unbearable sorrows. After Christ was resurrected, He sent us the Great Comforter, God the Holy Spirit, to dwell within us and give us the "peace that passes all understanding" in the time of our greatest needs (Php 4:7). The Lord has not left us alone or lonely. He is there every step of the way. We only have to call out His name, and He will be there.

As Christians, we have blessed assurance from the Almighty God that we will be reunited with our loved ones in Heaven. Michael had that assurance. So do his parents. The Lord has promised—that we can depend on. As Christians, when we leave this earth, our spirits go to be with our Lord and Creator where we are gathered together in His name. Death is not the end. It is only the beginning...

In loving memory:

Michael William Renner

June 27, 1990 ✝ March 2, 2010

Bible Study: Job 42:9-17; Psa 34:18, 139:13-16; Pro 3:5; Ecc 12:1-14; Isa 41:10; Isa 66:13; Jer 1:5; Lam 3:22-26; Mat 5:4, 18:14, 19:14; Joh 14:1-4; Rom 5:1-21, 8:18-28; 2Co 1:3-4, 5:1-21; Php 2:11-13, 4:7-8; Rev 22:16-17.

In Memory of Michael

It was still early when the shock of death awakened us.
The news was too much to bear—
our nephew, Michael, was gone.
Spring was somewhat in the air, but not quite there.
I remember the cherry trees were in bloom.
And, too, I recall seeing snow falling in sunshine.

In morning shadows, the family gathered
amid smells of coffee brewing and bacon cooking.
All was too surreal. Time seemed to stand still.
Sorrow floated like ashes and settled on shoulders
as boxes filled with flashes of photographic memories
were brought out for all to see.

Michael's shimmering silver drums sat in a vacuous silence.
Only the chimes of the Grandfather clock now marked time.
His guitar leaned against the wall by the hall.
Blue ribbons and metallic trophies on shelves told the story
of a life once filled with accomplishments and budding glory.

There were so many expressions of sympathy shared—
with loving embraces and kind faces
offering up words of prayer.
But there was no comfort there.
Worse still, it was clear time would not heal—
no matter what they say.
Reality is shrill.
Snakes bite. Venomous snakes kill.
It's the same with that whole array of colored pills.

The Good News is life does go on.
The sun sets. The sun also rises.[1]
Life is not in past tense. Our present rests in future tense.
One life ends. Another begins.
Michael's spirit has returned to our Heavenly Father Who sent it.
This blessed assurance is the one true consolation.

We will miss you, Michael. Go with God.

1. Ecc 1:5.

Suffer the little children to come unto me...for of such is the kingdom of God. (Mar 10:14)

The LORD is my shepherd; I shall not want. He maketh me to lie down in green pastures: he leadeth me beside the still waters...Yea, though I walk through the valley of the shadow of death, I will fear no evil: for thou art with me...I will dwell in the house of the LORD forever. (Psa 23:1-2, 4, 6)

The pain and sorrow parents bare in the loss of a child is utterly devastating. The anguish and suffering can be even more amplified if the tragedy is a horrendous accident. In the mortal realm, there is no comfort or consolation. But, as Christians, we have been given "a peace that passes all understanding" through Jesus Christ, our Lord (Php 4:7).

To be sure, as Christians, we are not always shielded from suffering or loss. Jesus Himself said "the rain falls on the just and on the unjust." (Mat 5:45). He never promised we would not be without tribulation in our lives. He did promise, however, he would "never leave us nor forsake us" (Heb 13:5). In other words, He will never leave us alone in our suffering. He will always be there with us in any and all circumstances, and He will bring us peace and comfort like no other. All we need do is call out His name, and He will be there.

This is the blessed assurance we have in Christ, and it is never more evident than in the darkest moments of our lives. Our Lord is not a distant, faraway God. Through the indwelling Holy Spirit, He remains up close and personal and will see us through any and all circumstances. We can be assured no matter what tragedy befalls us in this life, the Lord will be there to carry us through, giving us comfort in time of sorrow, strength to endure, and the ability to go on.

Even more importantly, through our faith in Christ Jesus, there remains hope for a most perfect and beautiful eternal life in the hereafter and that, one day, we will be together again with our loved ones where there is no pain, suffering, or sorrow. The Lord has promised us this, and we can count on it. It is all there in His Word.

In loving memory:

Chad Allen Smith

May 3, 1994 ✞ May 27, 2012

Matthew Scott Tribby

August 9, 1999 ✞ December 27, 2008

Bible Study: Psa 23:1-6, 48:14, 68:20; Mar 10:14; Act 2:21; Rom 5:17, 8:2, 21, 28, 38; 1Co 1:22; Php 1:20, 4:1-7; 2Ti 2:10; Heb 13:5; 1Jo 3:14.

Sweet, Sweet Child,
Go Now With God

Green pastures. Still waters.
The table was set and prepared long ago.
We just didn't know. How could we?
In the midst of tears, we falter.
Still, we lay him at your altar, Lord.
He is yours. He has returned to you.
You have called him home to rest.

He is gone now, but will never be forgotten.
When we think of him, we will think of his loving heart,
his sweet, gentle nature, and his winning smile.
You gave him to us, dear Lord, for such a short while,
and, in that time, we were blessed so very much.

Before the foundations of the world,
You named him in your Book of Life.
With this blessed assurance from you, our Christ,
we now lay him down and pray.
We know, Sweet Jesus,
he is with you this very day,
safe in your arms to stay.

Sweet, sweet child, go now with God.

According to my earnest expectation and my hope, that in nothing I shall be ashamed, but that with all boldness, as always, so now also Christ shall be magnified in my body, whether it be by life, or by death. For to me to live is Christ, and to die is gain. (Php 1:20-21)

I wrote this poem as a memorial to my sister-in-law, Ginger Salvesen. She didn't find the Lord until later in life, but after she was saved, she had a fire and passion for serving Him. It wasn't always easy, for she had a lot of sickness in her last years. And, like all of us, she didn't always get it right, but that was okay, for she loved the Lord with all her heart. Jesus understands and expects we will stumble along life's pathway, but He loves us just the same and unconditionally. Once we have asked Him into our heart with sincerity and conviction, there is nothing we can do that will cause Him to reject us. He loves us so much that He is willing to forgive all our faults and foibles and to cover us in His own righteousness.

Death is the finality of this finite vessel called our body. One day this earthly vessel will perish. None of us knows when, but each of us will have to face that final reality one day. When we are young, we don't think too much about death unless we have had an event in life that makes us aware of how temporary life can really be. But, when we are old, we think about it daily. As the clock ticks off the seconds, minutes, and hours, we tend to conserve our time in old age, as well as narrow our focus on what is important. The unchanging fact is one day each of us will have to walk through "the valley of the shadow." We need to prepare to ensure we will be walking through the right door and that Christ will be walking with us so we can live with Him for eternity in Heaven.

There is only one way to do that. That's what Jesus taught when He was on this earth. He said: "...I am the way, the truth, and the life: no man cometh unto the Father, but by me" (Joh 14:6). The only way through Heaven's door is to accept Jesus into your heart before you die, to ask Him to forgive your sins, and to receive the Grace He alone can offer. He paid a high price on the Cross at Calvary so those of us who accept His Grace will live with Him for Eternity. Our only requirement is to acknowledge Who He is and why He came to earth. It's so simple. Yet, it will make all the difference for you in Eternity.

It has been several years since Ginger passed on to be with the Lord, but I still miss her. Yet, I know where she is, and I know we will meet again in Heaven. Won't you call on Jesus today and ask Him into your heart? Join us so we will all be together in Glory one day.

In loving memory:

Virginia Carol Adams Anderson Salvesen

January 6, 1938 ✝ February 8, 2009

Bible Study: Job 14:14-16; Psa 16:11, 21:4-6, 39:1-7; Pro 11:30-31; Isa 25:8; Dan 12:2-3; Mat 7:13-14, 19:29, 22:32; Mar 10:30; Luk 18:18, 30; Joh 3:16-17, 4:14, 35-36, 6:51-69, 8:51, 10:10, 14:6; 1Co 15:20-26; 2Co 4:17; 2Ti 2:10; Gal 2:20, 6:8; Eph 1:3-14; 2:8-10; Col 3:4; 1Pe 5:4; 1Jo 1:1-2, 2:20-25, 5:13-20; Rev 3:5-8, 21:4.

A Prayer for You

Today I faced Death,
just like the poet described the early morning fog.
It crept in softly "on little cat's feet."[1]
It was then the Lord took me away gently
before anyone knew I was gone.

It wasn't the going that was so bad
or even not knowing "Why."
The hardest part of all was saying "Goodbye."

The "What" was pretty much a given.
There was no doubt.
My body simply gave out.
My spirit then returned to the Creator,
to our Savior, our Maker—the Lord Jesus Christ.

I had hoped the "When" would be in my old age,
at the end of a long and fruitful life.
And it was.

I had hoped the "Where" would be a place
surrounded by family and friends.
And it was.

I had hoped the "How" would come softly and tenderly,
as though I had fallen asleep.
And it did.

This day I walked through the valley of the shadow,
and I'm now in the most perfect place
of boundless beauty and eternal grace,
for I have come face to face with my Lord.

Long ago, I made my choice to be here with Him—
long before Death crept in,
and, it has made all the difference.
I want you all to have the same blessed assurance.
This is my prayer for you.

1. Excerpt from the poem: *Fog* by Carl Sandburg, in his book *Chicago Poems*, 1916.

Celebration

Alleluia! Christ Is Come!

And after these things I heard a great voice of much people in heaven, saying, Alleluia; Salvation, and glory, and honour, and power, unto the Lord our God: For true and righteous are his judgments...

And the four and twenty elders and the four beasts fell down and worshipped God that sat on the throne, saying, Amen; Alleluia. And a voice came out of the throne, saying, Praise our God, all ye his servants, and ye that fear him, both small and great.

And I heard as it were the voice of a great multitude, and as the voice of many waters, and as the voice of mighty thunderings, saying, Alleluia: for the Lord God omnipotent reigneth.

Let us be glad and rejoice, and give honour to him: for the marriage of the Lamb is come, and his wife hath made herself ready.

And to her was granted that she should be arrayed in fine linen, clean and white: for the fine linen is the righteousness of saints.

And he saith unto me, Write, Blessed are they which are called unto the marriage supper of the Lamb. And he saith unto me, These are the true sayings of God. (Rev 19: 1-2, 4-9)

The Dining Room Table

[Jesus said:] Come, ye blessed of my Father, inherit the kingdom prepared for you from the foundation of the world: For I was an hungred, and ye gave me meat: I was thirsty, and ye gave me drink: I was a stranger, and ye took me in: Naked, and ye clothed me: I was sick, and ye visited me: I was in prison, and ye came unto me...Verily I say unto you, Inasmuch as ye have done it unto one of the least of these my brethren, ye have done it unto me. (Mat 25:34-36, 40)

Reflecting one Christmas on the "Reason for the Season," I thought about a certain Christian woman who had a great impact on my life even though I never had the privilege of meeting her. She was born before the turn of the 20th Century and lived through WWI and most of the Depression. At age six, she and her five-year-old sister were orphaned. Together, they spent a good deal of their childhood working in a boarding house.

There, they washed dishes, cleared the table, and did housework in exchange for their keep. At the beginning, they were so small the proprietor had to make a step bench for them to reach the kitchen sink. They never sat at the long, fancy table in the dining room to eat. They weren't even allowed to sit at the kitchen table. Instead, they sat on the floor in the corner of the kitchen by the stove with their plates on their laps.

As an adult, this Christian lady was always offering a helping hand to those in need. When a relative returned from WWI with mustard gas poisoning, the lady brought him into her home and nursed him with loving care until he died. When her sister was diagnosed with cancer, she did the same and then took her sister's son, Charlie, as her own. Over the years, she took in several children that had no place to go.

Sometimes, there was no money for presents at Christmas time, but they always made do with what they had. This sweet lady made sure those in her household were clothed and well fed. All the while, she willingly shared with others and helped out when she could. Like the widow in the Bible, God always provided enough to get them through each day.

The whole family was very musical and over time acquired a piano and a guitar. On many an evening, there was lots of good old-fashioned gospel music to be heard throughout the neighborhood emanating from the family's front parlor. Through the years, the lady and her family were a continual source of love, joy, and comfort to their community.

My father once told me the story of coming to her house for the first time when he was eight years old to visit his friend, Charlie. This precious lady invited him to sit at her kitchen table and gave him a full meal with two homemade biscuits right out the oven and a bowl of rice and butter beans hot off the stove. While he ate, she sewed a button on his shirt. Then, before he left, she presented him with a neat pile of freshly washed and pressed clothes that were just the right size. For a boy who wore only raggedy hand-me-downs and whose stomach gnawed most all the time from hunger, this meant the world to him. He became a regular visitor to this warm and inviting household.

That lady was my grandmother—Carrie Francis Campbell Roberts. She died at age 42 of cancer long before I was born. She never traveled very far from her hometown of Columbia, South Carolina. She only had a grade school education and never attained any great success. She worked in a textile mill most all her life and ran a boarding house with her mother-in-law,

Suzanne Roberts, mostly taking in those who couldn't pay. She raised four fine Christian children, two sons and two daughters, along with two other children, Charlie, her late sister's son, and Estine, her daughters' friend who didn't have a home. All this she did without help from her absentee husband. There were many other children, too, that she took in and cared for temporarily when they were in need.

When she died, she didn't have much money. She didn't even own a home. Yet, all my life, time and again, when I met anyone who had known her, they would say: "Your Gran'ma Carrie was the finest lady I ever knew, and I will never forget what she did for me." My father was one of those people. When he grew up, he married her youngest daughter—my mother.

It's so easy for us as Christians to forget that, even though Christ's sacrifice was for the whole world, He's only looking for those who are repentant and pliable and who are willing to give their whole heart to Him. In return for all He did for us, the best way we can show our gratefulness and love to Him is by keeping His commandments and loving others unconditionally with a spirit of selfless giving—like my grandmother did.

The Lord's not looking for those with pedigrees or those expecting to be first in the Kingdom because of their religious affiliations, bloodlines, worldly status—or even their "good" works. No, none of that will get you one foot through Heaven's door. The Lord wants your heart—your whole heart and nothing less will do. He doesn't care how much money you have or your position in the community. He doesn't care one bit about where you came from. He's more concerned with the state of your heart and which way you're going when you reach eternity. That's why it's so important for each of us to define our lives while here on this earth and live accordingly—not unto ourselves, but unto the Lord.

If she could, my grandmother might tell us something like this of what it will be like in Heaven:

> I was among those in rags and tatters who were invited to Christ's wedding feast. When I was still just a little girl, the Lord cleaned me up and invited me to His table, and I accepted whole-heartedly. Those like me who may appear to be no one and of no worth in this earthly world are everything to the Lord. All I had to do was ask Him to come into my heart, and He did.
>
> Years later, when I arrived in Heaven for the Wedding Feast, Jesus lightly touched my shoulder and simply said, "Welcome, friend." I don't recall He ever asked me even once about anything concerning my genealogy—who my parents were or where I came from. He didn't ask me about my profession or what talents I brought to the table. He didn't even ask if I had ever broken any of His commandments. You see, He had already forgiven all my sins when I first asked Him to come into my heart as a little girl.
>
> At first, there in that great Heavenly Hallway, there was no one but the Lord and me. It was then He had asked if I knew Who He was. When He did, I went down on my knees, for I felt so unworthy to be in His presence. I was so overcome I couldn't say anything. With my head bowed, I just nodded and began to sob. He pulled me up gently and put His arms around me.
>
> "Here, little lady," He said, "Sit with me at my table. Eat. Drink. Take your fill. Bathe in my living baptismal waters, and I will clothe you in the white robes of My righteousness. Come and stay here with me forever." And, I did.

When Christ brought me into His Kingdom, He dressed me in His righteousness and placed me at His table as one among many of His closest friends. It was then I thought back to my childhood when the boarders would argue over who would sit at the head of that long, wooden table. All the while, my sister and I were wishing we could simply be allowed the privilege of sitting anywhere at the table and enjoying the freshly prepared food. Instead, we ate the leftovers while huddled on the floor by the kitchen stove. It wouldn't have mattered to us where we sat at that table. We just wanted to be included.

Now, here in this Heavenly place, I was thrilled to be in the Lord's presence and to be among those invited to His majestic table. Still, I was so scared and so in awe that I didn't open my eyes at first. When I finally did, I had to smile. In fact, I almost laughed out loud, for, you see, there before me were thousands of wide, broad, and perfectly *round* tables with people of all races and from all walks of life sitting around them, and there was Jesus leisurely strolling about visiting with each and every one. I recognized some as those I had helped along the way and whom I had invited to my own kitchen table. All were dressed the same—in white robes—and all were enjoying the same portions. In God's house, everyone is treated equally. No one sits at the head of the table, and no one is ever left out!

We continued there for a long while, all feasting together in one accord. High and lifted up was the Lord's throne with His cherubim and seraphim keeping watch. My God! He is magnificent!

To my big brother, Stan, with much affection and love and to his family as well:
Michael, Jeanie, Patrick Sean and wife Michele,
and grandchildren Jay, Reva, James, Lauren, Taylor, and Ryan.

The oldest of Grandma Carrie's grandchildren, Stan was the only grandchild
out of the eighteen to know her, for she helped raise him from birth.
He was five when she passed on in February 1938.

The voice said, 'Cry.' And he said, 'What shall I cry? (Isa 40:6)

...For all flesh is as grass, and all the glory of man as the flower of grass. The grass withereth, and the flower thereof falleth away: But the word of the Lord endureth for ever... (1Pe 1:24-25)

...And he that sat upon the throne said, 'Behold, I make all things new.' And he said unto me, 'Write: for these words are true and faithful.' (Rev 21:5)

...Arise, shine; for thy light is come, and the glory of the LORD is risen upon thee. (Isa 60:1)

In contrast to my poem, "Transcendence: Out of Darkness," which emphasizes man's spiritual condition preceding Christ's sacrifice on the Cross, as well as His ultimate victory over the Darkness, "Morning Glory" spotlights what is awaiting us in the full brightness of Christ's Return. Here, all darkness is past and all believers have been gathered to the Lord.

In this poem, I included the element of God's holy children as flowers. Isaiah sometimes used the descriptive metaphor of "flowers among the grass" to describe people, i.e. "grass" as the children of the world (the unsaved) and "flowers" as God's holy children (the saved). It is such a beautiful biblical illustration of how we as Christians blossom and grow into diverse, multi-colored flowers to be picked for "God's heavenly bouquet" when we remain in His light.

The multihued flowers also highlight the many blessings the Lord pours down on us, giving us our own unique qualities and shades of vibrant coloring in our distinct personalities and temperaments. Without a doubt, we can look forward to eternal splendor in Heaven when we stand before our Lord and King "on mirrored, golden glass."

With love and affection to Christina, Cindy, and Patricia Lorraine,
my "daughters in the faith." They are beautiful flowers selected for
Christ's heavenly bouquet and each holds a special place in my heart.

I know the beauty of the Lord by His flowers.

Bible Study: Exo 25:31-37; Psa 103:15-19; Sos 2:1; Isa 6:1, 3, 40:6; Mar 14:27-28; Luk 24:4-6; Joh 2:22, 21:14; Rom 8:34-39; 1Co 15:20-27; Col 2:12-16, 3:1; Jam 1:11-17; Rev 4:6, 8-11, 15:2, 22:12-14, 16-17, 20.

Morning Glory

A thousand years is but a single day
in the Father's heavenly bouquet,
all created in His own image.

Can you see the multi-colored diversity of our beings?
Yellow daffodils in a spring chill.
Wine-colored roses of Sharon.
White lilies of the valley.
Purple heather on the hill.

Yet still, while this old world remains,
its temporal grasses grow,
the flowers bloom, the flowers fade, and will *until*—

At one magnificent moment in time,
light fills the earth's darkest shadows
with Morning Glory.
Holy! Holy! Holy!
Grace be given by the Father, Son, and Spirit.

Can you imagine?
In that day, in a twinkling of an eye,
these flowers that have grown among the grass
will be transformed onto mirrored, golden glass,
blossoming into a glorious array
of God's celestial display.

On earth, the mountains resound in full chorus.
The Spirit takes wing. Birds sing. Bells ring.
Why such rapture? Why such rejoicing?
Did you not know? Have you not heard?
Long ago, the Black Knight was overthrown.
Sin and iniquity have been atoned.

The Good News has now spread
throughout the world:
"Christ has risen. The Son is risen."
When the Lord bids, "Come,"
Will you be ready for His return?

Epilogue

KING of Kings and LORD of Lords

And one of the elders saith unto me, Weep not: behold, the Lion of the tribe of Judah, the Root of David, hath prevailed to open the book, and to loose the seven seals thereof. (Rev 5:5)

* * *

And I saw heaven opened, and behold a white horse; and he that sat upon him was called Faithful and True…and his name is called The Word of God. And the armies which were in heaven followed him upon white horses…And he hath on his vesture and on his thigh a name written, King Of Kings, And Lord Of Lords. (Rev 19:11-16)

Jesus Is Calling: What Is Your Answer?

[Jesus said]: Come unto me, all ye that labour and are heavy laden, and I will give you rest...If any man will come after me, let him deny himself, and take up his cross, and follow me... Behold, thy King cometh unto thee, meek, and sitting upon an ass, and a colt the foal of an ass...For I say unto you, Ye shall not see me henceforth, till ye shall say, Blessed is he that cometh in the name of the Lord. (Mat 11:28, 16:24, 21:5, 23:39)

As the world goes whirling by, our individual lives continue, with everyone going about their business as usual. Unless faced with a crisis or even death itself, most aren't acutely aware of just how quickly their lives are passing. The fact remains time is running out for each and every individual on this planet. We are only allotted so many years here on earth and then we die. We need to be prepared for that. Even more importantly, we need to be prepared for what happens *after* we die.

One of my favorite quotes is from Shakespeare's Hamlet. He said: "There are more things in heaven and earth, Horatio, than are dreamt of in your philosophy."[1] In other words, we can't even begin to fathom what is in this earth, much less what is in Heaven.

The Apostle Paul said it another way: "For now we see through a glass, darkly; but then face to face..." (1Co 13:12). He goes on to say what we see in the natural is not all there is. Indeed, there is a spiritual "covering"—like a "film" or "smoke"—that obscures those things of the spirit he calls "the unseen" (2Co 4:18). This covering will remain in place while we are here in the natural, making it impossible for us to see what's on the "other side."

That said, there *is* someone who can see each of us clearly through this "veil." Matter of fact, He can see down to our innermost being and knows our every thought. That "Someone" is God. We've been introduced to Him as the Second Personage of the Godhead—the Lord and Savior, Jesus Christ of Nazareth.

We know from the Bible that Jesus died on the Cross at Calvary so that everyone who will repent and ask forgiveness for their sins can be saved by His Grace. It doesn't matter how great the sin—Jesus is always merciful to forgive. If you trust Him completely and have faith in Him, He will take you safely to the other side when you die. There, you will live with Him forever in Heaven. It seems simple enough. Yet, sadly, the Bible says many people will reject this magnanimous offer.

The question for you is this: If you were to die today, are you prepared for what's ahead on the other side? Have you asked the Lord into your heart so you can live with Him in eternity? If not, will you accept His free gift of grace and salvation? Will you say "Yes" right now—this very minute—while you are still on this earth? *It will be too late after you die.* You see, the Lord says He will accept us on faith only while we are here on earth in the physical, for it is written: "It is appointed unto men once to die, but after this the judgment..." (Heb 9:27).

The Lord has given you free will to decide. You can either *accept* Him or *reject* Him. Which will you choose? Good or evil? Life or death? Heaven or hell? It's entirely up to you!

Can't you hear Him calling? *Jesus is calling you.* But, He won't wait forever. What is your answer?

---

1. From the play *Hamlet*, Act 1, scene v by William Shakespeare

And the Lord went before them by day in a pillar of a cloud... (Exo 13:21)

...behold, the Lion of the tribe of Judah, the Root of David, hath prevailed... (Rev 5:5)

...To him that overcometh will I give to eat of the tree of life, which is in the midst of the paradise of God. (Rev 2:7)

There is none holy as the LORD: for there is none beside thee: neither is there any rock like our God... (1Sa 2:2) ...In the beginning was the Word, and the Word was with God, and the Word was God. (Joh 1:1)

...And when the seven thunders had uttered their voices, I was about to write: and I heard a voice from heaven... (Rev 10:4)

Before this book went to press, one of my favorite nieces, Denise Anne Smith, for whom I had dedicated this poem, died quite suddenly at age 60. She was such a sweet person and devout and faithful Christian. We lived far apart and never got to see each other in later years, but we talked on the phone now and again. In those times, we had good conversations about the Lord. The importance of following Christ and not being led astray by the different religions and philosophies of this world and what the Bible says about this was among our many topics. Denise had a big heart for keeping people "on track" for Jesus. This is why I dedicated this poem especially to her. She is now resting in the arms of our Lord and Savior. We will miss her.

The Bible tells us the way of the Lord is a very narrow one and "few there be that find it" (Mat 7:14). No matter what your teachers or even some preachers tell you, you cannot mix Christianity with any other philosophy or religion. For sure, you will not find the Lord in any other belief system, for we are justified by faith alone in Christ alone (Psa 148:13, Jde 1:4). Mixing your Christian faith with any other belief is a recipe for spiritual disaster. The Lord came to save everyone on this planet who would choose Him alone. But, if you are looking for the Lord in all the wrong places, you will never get to the point where you can make that choice. First, you have to *know* Him and know Who He is in the Trinity that is God.

In loving memory of my niece:

Denise Anne Smith

July 6, 1956 ✝ July 31, 2016

"We have come with open hearts... O, let the ancient words impart."
—From *Ancient Words,* Song By Michael W. Smith

Bible Study: Gen 2:9; Exo 3:14, 13:21, 17:6; Deu 32:13-15, 31; 2Sa 22:11; Psa 18: 2, 10, 31, 46, 28:1, 31:3, 46:10, 56:8, 62:1-7, 71:3, 78:35, 83:18, 86:10, 92:15, 94:22, 95:1, 104:3; Isa 2:2, 8:14, 12:4, 17:10, 42:8, 43:10-13, 44:24; Mat 23:37-39, 24:30; Mar 14:27-28, 61-64; Luk 6:45, 20:17, 23:33; Joh 1:1, 14, 3:8, 10:7-9, 14:6; Act 2:2, 4:11; Rom 9:33, 10:8-18; 1Co 10:4; Eph 2:20; 1Jo 5:20; 1Pe 2:6-8; Rev 2:7, 5:5, 10:3-4, 12:14, 22:2, 14.

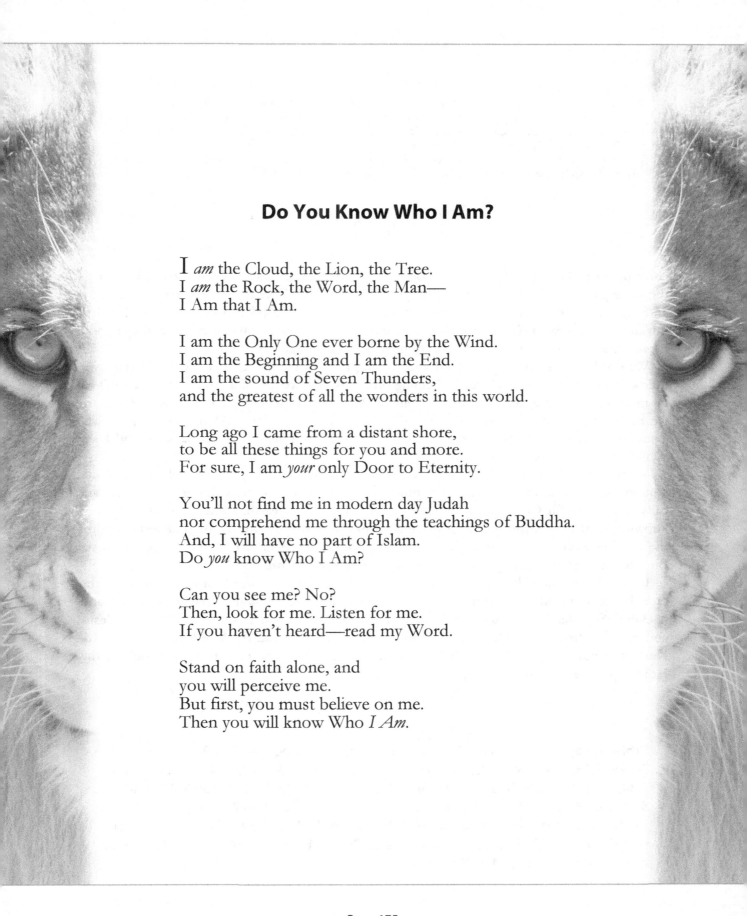

Do You Know Who I Am?

I *am* the Cloud, the Lion, the Tree.
I *am* the Rock, the Word, the Man—
I Am that I Am.

I am the Only One ever borne by the Wind.
I am the Beginning and I am the End.
I am the sound of Seven Thunders,
and the greatest of all the wonders in this world.

Long ago I came from a distant shore,
to be all these things for you and more.
For sure, I am *your* only Door to Eternity.

You'll not find me in modern day Judah
nor comprehend me through the teachings of Buddha.
And, I will have no part of Islam.
Do *you* know Who I Am?

Can you see me? No?
Then, look for me. Listen for me.
If you haven't heard—read my Word.

Stand on faith alone, and
you will perceive me.
But first, you must believe on me.
Then you will know Who *I Am*.

Wherefore seeing we also are compassed about with so great a cloud of witnesses, let us lay aside every weight, and the sin which doth so easily beset us, and let us run with patience the race that is set before us, looking unto Jesus the author and finisher of our faith; who for the joy that was set before him endured the cross, despising the shame, and is set down at the right hand of the throne of God. For consider him that endured such contradiction of sinners against himself, lest ye be wearied and faint in your minds. (Heb 12:1-3)

This poem is the sequel I wrote to "Follow the Horses: The Quest." Once again I looked to the Bible passage referring to the Lord's spiritual "horses" in Zechariah—where they are going and why. When we go before the Lord, we will want to give a good answer as to how we spent our time on this earth. We should be like Paul and keep our eye on the prize—running a good race all the way to the end (1Co 9:24). In this way, we will find "rest" in Him.

We do that by studying the Word and sharing the Gospel any chance we get in our own little corner of the world, as well as helping others as best we can along life's way. We can't all be missionaries and evangelists, but we can all share our knowledge of the Savior with those we meet, and we can try to live our lives as a testimony to Him. Along the way, we will sometimes get thrown from our horse, but that's okay as long as we get back on and keep racing toward the "mark" that is Christ.

We're not in the race with anyone else. We're in a race with time, and we only have a finite amount of it. As soon as we are born, time starts running out. Our goal, our "prize," as Paul calls it, is to fulfill God's purpose while we're here on this earth, sometimes without even knowing what that purpose is. But, if we keep praying, studying the Word, and seeking Him, the Lord will reveal what He expects us to accomplish and will give us the means to do so. But, the first priority is to *answer the call*—the high calling of Christ.

Can you hear the tick, tick, tock of the clock? If you haven't already, it's time to get in the race. It's time to move out and get going. It's never too late—as long as you're still alive and "ticking." So, what are you waiting for? Get in the race and run as fast as you can toward Jesus and *not* away from Him. He is your answer for all Eternity. Read the Word. Study the Word. Know the Word. Through it all, let go of the reins and hold on tight to the "mane" of the Holy Spirit. He will direct your path.

Bible Study: Gen: 3:16; Isa 9, 53; Psa 19:5; Ecc 9:11; Zec 1:7-11, 4:2, 6:1-8; Mat 1:1, 20-25, 2:15, 4:3-4, 8:20, 9:6, 11:27; Mar 1:1, 2:28, 8:31, 9:7-12; Luk 1:32, 3:22, 4:41, 7:34, 8:28, 9:22-56, 10:22, 18:8; Joh 1:18, 34, 49, 51, 3:16, 35-36, 5:19-27, 6:40-42, 53-69, 8:28-36, 12:23-24, 13:31, 14:13, 17:1-12, 20:31, 21:15-17; Rom 3-9, 5:10, 8:3, 29-32, 12:2; 1Co 9:24, 15:28; Gal 2:20, 4:4-7; Eph 4:13; Phil 2:15; Col 1:13; 1Th 1:10; Heb 1:2-8, 2:6-10, 3:6, 5:5-8, 7:28; 2Pe 1:17; 1Jo 1:3-7, 2:22-23, 3:1-8, 23, 4:9-15; 2Jo 1:9; Rev 1:13, 5:9, 14:4, 21:7.

Follow the Horses: The Race

I am off again to begin another visionary journey
to follow the horses through the Ancient Book
and take a closer look at its hallowed pages.
We are one, my horse and I,
as the modern world goes whirling by,
now becoming just a blur under
the darkening Western Sky.

Once again, we follow these celestial creatures
through the corridors of time
in all their powerful energy,
presented in a Word-perfected synergy
of fluid imagery and flowing rhyme.

We follow the horses racing,
over fields, farms, and prairies.
We follow the horses wading
through streams, rivers, and rapids.

We pass horses shackled and bridled,
plowing, plodding, pulling.
We pass horses free and unfettered,
Galloping, trotting, prancing.
We see horses in constant motion,
leaping, bucking, jumping, dancing.

I lean in as my horse follows after
the Wings of the Wind.
I hold on, his mane clasped tightly in my hands.
I ride high, my knees tensed against
the beefy muscles of his sides.

We do not stop, my horse and I.
We continue on.
We are now racing against time.
I whisper in my champion's ear.
What can you see, my boy?
What can you hear?

(Continued)

For the moment,
he is immersed in the intensity of the chase.
It is his role to keep pace with history.
And yet, for me, it all remains one great Mystery.

His focus is clearly on the race,
but I can see in the distance bright skies,
the Apostle's prize,
and the sun on the horizon.

Yet, still, close behind,
night shadows are moving in.
All around, I hear mourning doves,
thundering hooves,
and the sound of soldiers marching.

Then, through the din,
the Lord calls to me:
"Run, run!
Faster if you can.
The history of it all is catching up."

"You will make it,
as long as you follow my horses.
Don't look back.
Keep your eye on the horizon,
and look to the sun.
Always, look to the sun!
My One True Light is just beyond."

Sic Transit Tenebris[1]

Yea, the future, my child, is bright!
When the darkness comes,
it is simply the night.

What the shadows deplore
the Son will restore,
and the world will come back to the light.

1. [sik tran-zit ten-uh-bris] — *Thus Passes the Darkness*

END

And Jesus came and spake unto them, saying, All power is given unto me in heaven and in earth. Go ye therefore, and teach all nations, baptizing them in the name of the Father, and of the Son, and of the Holy Ghost: Teaching them to observe all things whatsoever I have commanded you: and, lo, I am with you always, even unto the end of the world. Amen. (Mat 28:18-20)

My God!
He Is Magnificent!

www.HeIsMagnificent.com

✳

Facebook.com/HeIsMagnificent

Printed in the United States
By Bookmasters